791.43

Critical Guides to Spanish and Latin American Texts and Films

72 Pedro Almodóvar

Critical Guides to Spanish and Latin American Texts and Films

EDITED BY ALAN DEYERMOND & STEPHEN HART

PEDRO ALMODÓVAR

Ann Davies

Lecturer in Spanish
Newcastle University

London
Grant & Cutler Ltd 2007

© Grant & Cutler Ltd 2007

ISBN: 978 0 7293 0452 8

Depósito legal: V. 4.946 - 2007

Front cover photo © El Deseo D.A., s.l.u./Paola Ardizzoni & Emilio Pereda

Printed in Spain by
Artes Gráficas Soler, S.A., Valencia
for
GRANT & CUTLER LTD
55–57 GREAT MARLBOROUGH STREET, LONDON W1F 7AY

Contents

To Sylvia Jenkins, who started all this.

Acknowledgements

Much of this book derives from my teaching of Almodóvar films. In this respect I cannot but acknowledge my former colleague Professor Chris Perriam, who worked with me on teaching Almodóvar and who illuminated much of my way. In what follows, any errors are due to me and not to him. I also owe a debt to the students at Newcastle University, at both undergraduate and postgraduate level, with whom it has been a great pleasure to look at all things Almodovarian. Grateful thanks also go to Mark Allinson, Jackie Collins, Jo Evans, Vanessa Knights and Rebecca Naughten, who have helped and informed me in various ways with this book.

Some of the material on *Matador* appeared previously in my article, 'The Spanish *Femme Fatale* and the Cinematic Negotiation of Spanishness', *Studies in Hispanic Cinemas* 1.1, (2004), 5–16. My thanks to the editors and to Intellect Press for permission to reproduce this material here.

1. Introduction

Pedro Almodóvar has become the dominant figure of contemporary Spanish cinema. The release of a new Almodóvar film in Spain is by now a major cultural event; and he was besieged by the press at Madrid airport on his return home from winning an Oscar for his 1999 film *Todo sobre mi madre*. Internationally he has become one of Spain's most successful cultural exports, and his films are taken to represent what Spanish film output as a whole is like, an expectation that his characteristic mixture of melodrama and offbeat comedy is what Spanish cinema in its entirety is all about. This equation of Almodóvar with Spanish film as a whole is not unproblematic in many ways, as we shall shortly see, and, while it speaks to Almodóvar's international success it is unfair in its lack of discernment of the uniqueness of his art. His work is, however, not without precedent in Spanish cinema, which has a strong history of comedy, while the popularity of folkloric musical film in Spanish cinema history has its counterpart in Almodóvar's use of Spanish and Latin American music as an integral part of and commentary on the unfolding story, culminating in the homage to Spanish film and singing star Sara Montiel in the director's 2004 film *La mala educación*.

Almodóvar's career spans Spain's democratic era after the death in 1975 of General Franco and the subsequent withering of the regime which Franco headed. Although Almodóvar's project has never been to accurately document Spanish history, his body of work offers some insights on both the highs and the lows of Spain's adjustment to democracy after years of Franco's dictatorship: its new found freedom reflected in his early films of madcap hedonism, its social travails in his later work that incorporates a look at such issues as urban deprivation and AIDS. And the common identification of him both as a gay director (although he himself has been reticent about his sexual preferences) and sympathetic towards women chimes in with the increasing recognition within Spanish society that both women and gay men must be treated with respect and as equals, in contrast to the repressive days of Francoism. Nonetheless, while Almodóvar is very much a director of his time and country, the radical changes in Spanish society and politics should not disguise Almodóvar's work as part of a continuum in popular Spanish film. Where he has been more successful than most Spanish directors, however, is his ability to bridge the divide that also characterised Spanish cinema until the contemporary democratic era, between popular film and film with aspirations to art, often interlaced with political allegory. The former is what people actually went to see in Spain, while the latter represented Spain abroad at film festivals and arthouse cinemas. Almodóvar's films manage to satisfy both camps.

This has not always made him popular with the Spanish film establishment. Almodóvar did not follow the career path through film school of most Spanish arthouse directors, instead learning his craft independently. His brand of filmmaking ran counter to government film policy of the 1980s, which favoured glossy, high-culture productions and costume dramas usually based on recognised literary classics, whereas Almodóvar's films emphasised contemporary urban life. The establishment, in the form of the Goya awards (Spain's equivalent of the Oscars) have twice snubbed Almodóvar's work, for *La ley del deseo* and *La mala educación*, as Marvin D'Lugo observes (2, p.59): D'Lugo conjectures that this arises from the fact that these two films are the only ones in Almodóvar's work to deal directly with homosexuality, but a more general critical distaste for Almodóvar's style (at the time of *La ley del deseo*) and phenomenal success (by the time of *La mala educación*) may also lie behind this. While some of this reaction may arise simply from pique at the success of an independent director who did not follow the establishment rule book, there are nonetheless reasons for disquiet at the pervasiveness of the Almodóvar phenomenon within Spanish cinema. Barry Jordan comments on Almodóvar's work in general that:

> Almodóvar's legacy [...] may not have been altogether positive or beneficial, in the eyes of domestic or foreign audiences. Indeed, the equating of 'Spanishness' with sex and sexual perversion (however playful and camp) may have reinforced some unhelpful, negatively stereotypical, perceptions of modern Spain and Spaniards.[1]

This possibility is undeniable, but the reason for this lies not so much with Almodóvar himself as with the ability of Spanish cinema to sell itself abroad as well as the willingness or reluctance of international audiences to extend their experience of Spanish culture beyond some amusing stereotypes. Almodóvar's success may well be a factor in the current emphasis on selling Spanish comedy to UK audiences.[2] Such comedies have not, however, had Almodóvar's success in making Spanish culture accessible to audiences elsewhere.

---

[1] Barry Jordan, 'How Spanish Is It? Spanish Cinema and National Identity', in *Contemporary Spanish Cultural Studies* ed. by Barry Jordan and Rikki Morgan-Tamosunas (London: Arnold, 2000), pp.68–78 (p.73).

[2] Some recent examples at the time of writing: *El otro lado de la cama* (Emilio Martínez Lázaro, 2002), *Di que sí* (Juan Calvo, 2004), *Seres queridos* (Dominic Harari and Teresa Pelegri, 2004).

Almodóvar has been influential on the Spanish and international scene in his development of a stable of actors who have
established themselves through his work. Above all, he brought to the
fore the actor Antonio Banderas, who gained attention through his
work in the director's early films and in particular *Mujeres al borde
de un ataque de nervios* which succeeded internationally as well as at
home. Subsequently Banderas has become a star in Hollywood as
well as Spain. At the domestic level, the actress Carmen Maura is
indelibly associated with Almodóvar: her return to his work with
Volver after a rift following *Mujeres al borde* has been widely
welcomed. More recently, Penélope Cruz has become associated
with his work (although she was well established before gaining
major roles in his films). Almodóvar has also collaborated with other
major actors of Hispanic cinema such as Assumpta Serna, Marisa
Paredes, Javier Bardem and Gael García Bernal, while actors such as
Chus Lampreave have followed long and strong career paths in
secondary roles in Almodóvar's films.

In many ways Almodóvar has become a star himself: often in
the credits we find, immediately after the title credit, the simple
phrase 'a film by Pedro Almodóvar' so that the director's credit
precedes that of the actors and implies that Almodóvar is more of a
commanding presence within his films than are his actors. In the
early years he performed small cameo roles in his own films (rather
as Alfred Hitchcock did in his): flamboyant cameos as a punk singer
in *Laberinto de pasiones* and a fashion designer in *Matador*, or more
low-key appearances such as an assistant in a hardware shop in *La
ley del deseo*. (His brother and producer Agustín Almodóvar has
appeared in such cameo roles in all the films, for instance as the
priest at a wedding in the more recent *Hable con ella*.) Although he
is no longer visible within the cinematic world he creates,
Almodóvar's worldview pervades his films so distinctively that in
itself it dominates the films as much as the individual performers of
the actors. People watch Almodóvar's films in expectation of the
heady mixture of melodramatic emotion, comedy, sexuality, colour
and sound that he presents to audiences time and again. Although, as
we have seen above, this offers the negative potential of depicting

Spain as no more as a hedonistic playground, it has nonetheless established the director as a maker of films that are both idiosyncratic and attractive.

In this sense it is easy to describe Almodóvar as an *auteur*. This term derives from early attempts in film theory (and notably by French film theorists, hence the use of a French word for the concept) to elevate cinema beyond its role simply as commerce and entertainment to that of artistic artefact on a par with the best novels, poems and paintings, virtually all of which have one author or guiding hand who expresses an individual perception and conception of the surrounding world and people. This individual vision supposedly persists across a range of works by the same person. In cinema, the work of the *auteur* would form a contrast to those directors who simply carried out a job of work, turning out a product meant primarily to entertain and to make money, without any artistic pretensions (known in this theoretical conception as *metteurs-en-scène*). This theory fell out of favour for a while, in part because films are not the same as books: the former require numerous personnel in order to be made; and the role of camera crew, lighting technicians, editors, scriptwriters, wardrobe and actors were increasingly recognised as contributing to the overall look and theme of the film. When we consider Almodóvar's own films we also have to bear this point in mind: he has had collaborators such as the group of actors with whom he surrounds himself, the composers of the music (notably Alberto Iglesias for the later films), the support of his brother as producer, and so on. The theory of the *auteur* has, however, returned in a modified form in recognition of the fact that the director may still link and orchestrate these collaborative elements into one whole. The director's name may also come to function as a label for a particular style of filmmaking, and in some cases a selling point (American directors Quentin Tarantino and Tim Burton exemplify this very well). Bearing the caveats about collaboration in mind, it is easy to consider Almodóvar as a remarkably consistent *auteur*.

Almodóvar's films return repeatedly to the same themes used for both comedy and drama. He is known as a woman's director: that is, he favours female characters and themes to do with women. In the majority of his films the female characters are the protagonists, functioning not as objects of desire that motivate the actions of others (men), but as subjects propelling their own narratives. We see things from their point of view. In doing this Almodóvar draws on earlier cinematic traditions such as the 1940s and 50s woman's film in the USA, a genre that explored women's emotional travails, but combines them with a contemporary European feel and touches of both modern and traditional Spanish society. Nor are the women of Almodóvar's films a collection of conventionally beautiful young women simply looking for the right man. He treats middle-aged and elderly women — often the butt of ridicule — with humour but also with gentleness, and has room for the more unconventional look, most notably that of actress Rossy de Palma, whose distinctive angular face has been applied to a varied range of Almodóvar's roles (a television presenter, a middle-class fiancée, a drug dealer, a maid, a housewife). As we shall see in subsequent chapters, particularly those dealing with the films *Mujeres al borde de un ataque de nervios* and *Todo sobre mi madre*, there is scope for reading more negative aspects into Almodóvar's insistence on female-centred narratives, in particular an occasional tendency to stress women as people driven primarily by emotions rather than rational thought, reminiscent of an age-old habit to think of women as less rational thinkers than men. In all his films without exception, Almodóvar considers not simply women but gender relations: how we conceive of what it is to be male or female and how the genders interact with each other. The director explores not only what it might mean to be a variety of different women — mother, lesbian, nun, transsexual, housewife, porn star, independent woman — but also delves into what it means to be male in contemporary Spain. While this may occur at a secondary level when the female characters are to the fore, Almodóvar has on occasion brought men to the centre of the screen and probed beneath conceptions of masculinity, as in *Carne trémula* and *Hable con ella*, for instance.

Almodóvar has also become known as a homosexual director, with somewhat less justification, as I discuss more fully in the next chapter on *Laberinto de pasiones*. Although the director is widely believed to be gay he himself is reticent about his sexual preferences, as noted earlier; but moreover his films deal with homosexuality surprisingly little (although some scholars observe a gay sensibility in his films: see *24, 26*). It is central to only two films, *Le ley del deseo* and *La mala educación* and crops up as a motif in *Laberinto* and *Matador*. Lesbian relationships also occur intermittently (for instance in *Pepi, Luci, Bom y otras chicas del montón, Entre tinieblas* and *Todo sobre mi madre*). Nonetheless Almodóvar treats sexualities alternative to the dominant heterosexual one in positive ways (that do not preclude critique), positioning all forms of sexuality as equal to each other with no need for comment. The only exception to this is the director's attacks on the selfishness and violence of heterosexual masculinity, as with the character of Iván in *Mujeres* and Sancho of *Carne trémula* (though even with the latter he prevents us from simple condemnation, as I discuss in the chapter on *Carne*). Sometimes the conflict between the sexes is treated in a light-hearted manner, and in fact Almodóvar has come in for some trouble on occasion when dealing with issues such as female abduction as in *¡Átame!*, in which the victim falls in love with her abductor; or rape, most notoriously in *Kika*, where a rape scene is played with strong comic elements (although the victim's subsequent trauma is duly acknowledged, it seems to have as much to do with the fact that the rape was televised as with the rape itself). Another motif that is less commonly noted by critics is Almodóvar's intermittent taste for sympathetic portrayals of psychopaths, as I shall discuss in more detail in the relevant films (*Matador* and *Hable con ella*). While these motifs allow us to look beyond simple stereotypes that allow for quick and easy condemnation (and thus dismissal), they nonetheless add an uncomfortable edge to some of Almodóvar's work.

In terms of style and genre, Almodóvar veers between comedy and melodrama, and usually within the same film. Some films are outright comedies (*Laberinto* and *Mujeres*), but most include highly charged scenes of melodramatic emotion; and this latter tendency has become more pronounced with the years. Almodóvar is also well known for his use of bright colour and of eccentric kitsch in costume, props and setting. His work is the opposite of restrained good taste. Indeed, Almodóvar can be seen as quite an iconoclastic director, cheerfully defying the very elliptical and allegorical style of Spanish cinema of the 60s and 70s, with its slow pace and muted lighting. During these years Spanish arthouse cinema appeared grey and melancholic, conveying to audiences the stagnation of the Franco years, and these artistic values persisted into the early democratic era. This is not to disparage these films, but it demonstrates the fresh air that Almodóvar's more colourful style breathed into Spanish cinema — or alternatively, what a shock it was those people who understood quality cinema in terms of high art and good taste.

To say that Almodóvar retains a unity of vision, theme and style as befits an *auteur* does not preclude the possibility that he has changed and developed in his approach to filmmaking. At the time of writing Almodóvar has directed sixteen feature films over twenty-five years, a remarkably productive output. As we shall see in more detail in the next chapter, the early films partake of the atmosphere of the *movida madrileña*, a flamboyant and hedonistic cultural style prevalent in Madrid shortly after the transition to democracy. The very early films (and in particular *Pepi, Luci, Bom*) are less polished owing to Almodóvar's inexperience and lack of funds, but they convey to us the pleasant giddiness of an era when the constrictive Francoist rule book was torn up and nothing had as yet arrived to replace it. The *joie de vivre* of these films nevertheless allows for the early appearance of Almodovarian melodrama, such as the sorrow and despair of the Mother Superior's ultimately unrequited love in *Entre tinieblas*. Almodóvar could also give a nod to other film styles such as gritty social realism in *¿Qué he hecho yo para merecer esto?* while still retaining elements of comic weirdness such as the little girl who can telekinetically wallpaper an entire kitchen in seconds. Gradually, however, the director became both more mainstream and more accessible to an international audience, reaching his first peak of success with the Oscar nomination for *Mujeres al borde de un ataque de nervios*. And in the mid-1990s, as Almodóvar grew older, the *movida* by now a distant memory, his films became more sober, more thoughtful. This new period started with *La flor de mi secreto* and has continued ever since. His films now touch on social issues, from political protest in *La flor* to child abuse in *Volver*; and while they retain the intricate plotting of films such as *Laberinto*, in which everything is related to everything else, the pace has now slowed. As we shall see in the chapters on *Carne trémula* and *Hable con ella* he began to treat male characters with all the complexities with which he had earlier treated women; and while his first films dealt with the Francoist past by simply ignoring it, some of the later films touch on history intermittently. He reached a second peak in 1999 with *Todo sobre mi madre*, which gained an Oscar for Best Foreign Language Film: by now he had become a major figure in European cinema. In an era in which the screening of foreign-language film on British television has become virtually non-existent, Almodóvar's films remain an exception, appearing intermittently on mainstream channels rather than being confined to the outer reaches of specialist satellite and cable channels. *Volver*, his latest film at the time of writing, has received considerable — and generally positive — attention from the mainstream media on its UK release.

About this book

Almodóvar's pre-eminence in contemporary Spanish cinema has been accompanied by assiduous critical attention, not only by reviewers and cultural commentators at home and abroad but also by academics. The selective bibliography at the back of the book is only an indication of the plethora of academic writings on the director: indeed, in November 2003 an entire academic conference in Cuenca was devoted to his work alone. In particular, two works have now become standard in Almodóvar criticism (and are duly cited in the bibliography at the back). Paul Julian Smith's seminal work *Desire Unlimited* (*3*) provides a searching film by film analysis of all the films as far as *Tacones lejanos* (with a subsequent edition adding review material on films as far as *Todo sobre mi madre*). Mark Allinson's *A Spanish Labyrinth* (*1*) also provides copious analysis but approaches the films thematically rather than chronologically.

In the space allowed a short Critical Guide such as this, a similar comprehensive survey of Almodóvar would be an impossible undertaking. Its intention is primarily to assist school and university students in their study of the director, and thus prefers to give an emphasis to those films most likely to be studied by such students. It functions as a selection of snapshots of Almodóvar's career rather than an extended chronological critique. Nonetheless the films selected should also provide an impression of how Almodóvar's work has changed over the course of time. However, many students of Almodóvar do not in the first instance set out to undertake comprehensive study of Almodóvar, but encounter him through one or two films; and their priority is often that exact film text. This guide aims to facilitate their study of such films. Its small size aims at ease of access.

Some omissions from Almodóvar's copious work have there-fore had to be made; and some omissions may seem more sinful than others. I particularly regret leaving out *La ley del deseo*. My reason for the omission was that his films of this period are already well covered with *Matador* and *Mujeres al borde de un ataque de nervios*. One reason why this omission may seem particularly large is the fact that for many years *La ley* was Almodóvar's only film that dealt specifically with homosexuality (until *La mala educación* joined it). But in some ways, though a discussion of this theme would be valuable, there is nonetheless a tendency to equate Almodóvar too simplistically with homosexuality, as is discussed in the next chapter. There is also a gap between *Mujeres al borde* and *Carne trémula* which I regret: these films, however, have never gained the attention of the mature films discussed here. While these missing films deserve more critical attention than they have received hitherto, here is not the place for it. This book concentrates on what we might consider the highlights of Almodóvar's career. If we think back to my earlier analogy of the book as a series of snapshots we can perhaps agree that, when looking at snapshots we tend to prefer those that show the subject in the best light. If throughout I have made my selection with the student primarily in mind, this is not to say that students should dismiss those films not covered. They also repay study, and are always worth watching for sheer pleasure.

2. *Laberinto de pasiones*

`The first film to be discussed in detail here, *Laberinto de pasiones* (1982), is a component part of Almodóvar's early films that ensured the director's eruption on to the Spanish cinema scene and laid the foundation for his reputation as a maker of crazy, gender-bending comedies, a label which continues to haunt discussion of Almodóvar's work, even though the aptness of the label may never perhaps have been complete. *Laberinto de pasiones* was Almodóvar's second film, after *Pepi, Luci, Bom y otras chicas del montón* (1980). As with *Pepi, Luci, Laberinto* was made at a time when Almodóvar was not yet part of the Spanish cinema establishment and did not have access to many resources, financial or otherwise, for making his film. Almodóvar made use of his friends such as Fabio McNamara as well as his own brother Agustín in a cameo role as an Islamic activist, and appears himself as film director and as punk star. The result is an occasionally makeshift film which nonetheless offers one of the highest numbers and widest range of characters in any of his films to date, and which shows a markedly more sophisticated approach from the previous *Pepi, Luci, Bom*.

These early films quickly provided Almodóvar with a cinematic calling card which indicated the styles and themes for which he would subsequently become famous: hedonism, outrageousness, and expressions of sexualities beyond the heterosexual norm (though as we shall see below, this last tag has its problems). And yet, while these styles and themes persist throughout Almodóvar's career of well over twenty years to a greater or lesser extent, *Laberinto* is very much a film of its time, deriving from a particular moment in Spanish cultural history which has since passed. The impact of that still resonates in contemporary culture, however, as the vibrant urban culture of the early 80s in Spain is revisited. For example, a recent film, *El calentito* (Chus Gutiérrez, 2005), attempts to capture this time, and inserts a sequence of *Laberinto* in its efforts to do so. For Almodóvar's films have become a crucial part of the memory of this era.

The *movida*

This cultural movement was known as the *movida madrileña* — usually abbreviated simply to the *movida* — that took place in the late 70s and early 80s, primarily in the Spanish capital. Almodóvar himself has argued that in fact the notion of the *movida* is an entity created by the media, that at the time those involved in the *movida* did not see themselves that way — but that there were nonetheless people working in that way in Madrid.[3] At any event, the label has come to stick, providing a shorthand for some of the cultural ideas being developed at the time: and Almodóvar's early films are now perceived as the quintessential evidence as to what the movement meant and means.

---

3 Nuria Vidal, *The Films of Pedro Almodóvar* (Madrid: Instituto de la Cinematografía y las Artes Audiovisuales, Ministerio de Cultura, 1988), p.37.

As Paul Julian Smith notes in his discussion on the film the *movida* may have drawn in part on the punk sensibilities coming from the UK and USA, but the root cause was very different: rather than, as in the UK case, a reaction to a grim situation (economic and employment problems), it derived from new cultural opportunities and possibilities (*3*, p.30) — indeed, a sense of freedom rather than entrapment. The *movida* was one example of the sense of release that came for many Spaniards after 1975 and the end of the right-wing dictatorship, headed by General Francisco Franco, that lasted nearly forty years. The dictatorship had fostered a sense of Catholic austerity and morality, stressing traditional gender roles, that increasingly sat ill with the political and cultural ferment of the 1960s that took place elsewhere in Europe, the growing prosperity of many Spaniards in a consumer society, and the political ideologies in the West at that time. As Spain underwent a transition to democracy (finally consolidated in 1982 with the handover of power from a right-wing government to a left-wing one), politics, society and culture experienced radical changes that gave release to the frustrations of many Spaniards, particularly the younger generation.

Not that politics or social concerns were of great import to those immersed in the *movida*. If we were to search for one word to summarise the movement, it would be tempting to choose hedonism. One prevailing notion of the *movida* was simply pleasure, and in particular pleasure in breaking the old rules of behaviour; so fashions became outrageous, people had recourse to various drugs, and the traditional notions in relation to sexuality and gender were blatantly flouted. This should not, however, divert us from the fact that the *movida* also witnessed a new surge of cultural creativity of which Almodóvar's early films were only a part. Both hedonistic pleasure and cultural production far outweighed political or social activism as a priority: the *movida* left the political transition to its own devices and simply 'dropped out'. These priorities were reflected in the *movida*'s cinema and certainly the early films of Almodóvar: if politics appeared at all it was simply to be parodied (as in the 'erecciones generales' of the previous *Pepi, Luci, Bom*). Almodóvar as director certainly did not follow the penchant of previous directors of the 60s and 70s with claims to be at the pinnacle of Spanish filmmaking, who used film to offer veiled critique of the Franco regime. While this might have arisen simply from the fact that the regime had just changed, leaving a vacuum as to what to critique, Almodóvar's films follow on rather from the more popular comedy films of the 70s, until recently less highly regarded by the critics if not the audiences, these comedies being more concerned even in the restrictive atmosphere of Francoism with risqué innuendo than political criticism. For the *movida* generation, politics was simply uninteresting, a hangover from the Franco days. Dropping out of the system, of course, is in itself a political statement of sorts, and we should treat the apparently wholesale rejection of politics with a certain amount of caution. What is significant for our purposes here is the break that Almodóvar would establish within quality Spanish cinema with the *nuevo cine español* of the 1960s, with its concerns for the faithful representation of the stagnation of Spanish life in the provinces, and its political allegory (allegory in order to evade the hand of Franco's censors), and his breach of the divide between art cinema and commercial cinema within Spain. The roots of that breach derive from the *movida*, and *Laberinto* gives us an early indication as to how Almodóvar would build on that breach in order to create his own unique brand of cinema to bridge the gap between popular and arthouse cinema. The wild party comedy we find in the film will remain in many of his later films, but attenuated, smoothed down to a finer gloss that will add to the commercial success of his comedy.

Madrid as setting and character

Almodóvar argues that the film functions as a 'rather ridiculous kind of glorification of Madrid […] which was what you saw in the media then. It's like a parody'.[4] If we accept this statement by Almodóvar, then a rather different light emerges as to the film being a true reflection of the *movida*: it is in fact sending the culture up to some degree. If the film is made partly to celebrate Madrid, and the

---

[4] Vidal, p.39.

cultural explosion of the *movida* (which, we should bear in mind, did not embrace all *madrileños* to the same degree), then Madrid becomes a composite character precisely made up of these people who wander in and out of the story. As critics have noted (see *4, 6*), the film is about Madrid as much as it is about the individuals whom we encounter as we watch the film. *Laberinto* is one of the few examples — and the most overt — of ensemble playing in Almodóvar's work: only the later *Mujeres al borde de un ataque de nervios* comes anywhere near the gallery of characters we find in *Laberinto*. Although the film's plot revolves primarily around the attempt to get together of Sexilia (Cecilia Roth) and Riza (Imanol Arias), their story is criss-crossed with that of other characters in a labyrinthine structure: the concept of the labyrinth is one we will look at below. As D'Lugo argues (*4*, p.130), Madrid becomes synonymous with the labyrinth of passions of the film. He comments that '[t]he foregrounding of the city [Madrid] as an assertion of a vibrant Spanish cultural identity is built around a rejection of the traditions that ordered Spanish social life for four decades' (p.125). He goes on to trace the historical figuring of the urban as an escape from the repression of the provinces in Spanish cinema of the 60s and 70s (pp.126–27) and suggests that in the early films Madrid is a place where characters come in order to find the freedom they do not find in other places (p.130).

The obvious sense of hedonism and 'anything goes' that is a fundamental part of the *movida* derives in part from a sense of collage, recycling cultural artefacts, making new cultures out of the bric-a-brac of the old. The Rastro flea market where the action starts, a familiar Madrid landmark, is a suitable opening setting and symbol for the film. The Rastro, offering its sense of life as a composite of disparate elements, forms the backdrop for Sexi and Riza as they casually cruise for men: their sex lives, too, consist of collage. Madrid itself comes to resemble this collage, made up of divergent characters with differing goals and desires, where one can reinvent oneself through second-hand resources. The character Queti (Marta Fernández-Muro) exemplifies this, using Sexi's clothes to transform herself. (Hence Sexi quickly overcomes her anger on seeing Queti dressed in her own clothes: it is all simply an integral part of the Madrid scene). Almodóvar argues for Queti as a kitsch character, drawing her ideas and resources from advice in popular magazines, which provide her with knowledge and a philosophy.[5] This philosophy she passes on to others, the girls in Sexi's band (against the backdrop of Sexi's room, with its mixture of colours and textures). Kitsch — the enjoyment of cultural forms that are usually acknowledged to be in bad taste — forms a running stylistic motif of Almodóvar's work, and we shall encounter it again in later films.

In particular we acquire a sense of crisscrossing personalities and sexualities, suggesting that both are interchangeable. From Riza's transformation into a punk singer, to Queti transforming herself by borrowing Sexi's clothes, to the checked shirt donned by Sexi after first going to bed with Riza that subsequently appears on Santi (Javier P. Grueso), the guitarist with whom Riza had a failed one-night stand — all suggest that characters can take up and discard, or even swap, identities and sexualities at will. The ultimate instance of this is when Queti finally replaces Sexi after surgery to remould her in Sexi's exact likeness: a conspiracy in which both women actively participate. All this contributes to the notion of Madrid and its people as simply a performance, theatre. People acquire and exchange multiple lives and personalities at will, symbolised in the reflection of many Rizas in the sunglasses hanging up for sale in the Rastro.

What does it mean, then, that in the end some of the characters leave Madrid, if Madrid is the centre of the *movida* and, as Riza is quoted as saying in the newspapers, it is where the action currently is? Our two central characters Riza and Sexi depart Madrid along with — not insignificantly — the band that served as Riza's passport to immersion in the *movida* itself. In a later section we shall see how Riza and Sexi's coming together in the film and departure from Madrid can be read on one level as a maturation of sexuality (although this is a reading that I will problematise): for now we could arguably view the departure from Madrid as a sign that the *movida* is simply a stage from which one must move on.

---

[5] Vidal, p.54.

Coincidence and the labyrinth

The labyrinthine nature of Madrid is expressed in the crisscrossing of characters and plotlines throughout the film, from the opening scene in the Rastro market where Riza and Sexi cruise past each other on the hunt for men: the intercutting between the two characters prefigures the fact that the two are each other's solution to the sexual problems that underlie their cruising. Riza reads a newspaper with headlines concerning both his own father and Sexi's, hinting at the connection between the two central characters and the two fathers, the latter together playing a part in the uncomfortable past that has resulted in Riza and Sexi's current cruising habits. The first ten minutes of the film introduce us to a variety of characters whose lives are interrelated but who walk past each other unaware of the significance, as in the sequence where the empress (Helga Liné), discovering that her stepson is in Madrid, makes a call from a Madrid phone box, behind which we see her stepson meet Sadec (Antonio Banderas). The jumble of scenes at the beginning of the film tends to confuse the viewer too, as we move to the Rastro, to Sexi's conversation with Susana (Ofelia Angélica), to the first flashback on the beach, then her father's conversation with the empress, another flashback (from his perspective this time), and then an apparently unconnected conversation between two unknown women. This last sequence is explained when Sexi's father (Fernando Vivanco) and the empress emerge into the room where the conversation is going on, so that we learn we are now in his waiting room. This last scene not only offers us a sidebar of comedy but also alerts us as to how to read the film's labyrinthine structure. We become aware that we need to hold the different plot threads together in our minds and be prepared to take up first one and then another as Almodóvar presents them in turn, in the knowledge that all these threads are interconnected. A later instance of how this works occurs later in the film when Queti gives beauty advice to band member Angustias (Concha Gregori): after some other scenes of greater import, Almodóvar inserts a vignette of Angustias rapidly taking Queti's advice as she realises that Ángel (Santiago Auserón), the man she secretly loves, is at her door. This incident is a small detail but shows how motifs disappear from one scene and turn up in another. The labyrinthine plot also develops in a meandering fashion. For example, when Eusebio (Ángel Alcázar), the singer who was rejected in favour of Riza, stands next to Sadec at a bus stop, the latter detects Riza's scent on him. We then cut to Sadec returning to his colleagues at the flat, where the scent he smelt on Eusebio will lead him another step towards uncovering Riza's true identity. The plot twists and turns picking up characters and following them, before dropping them for the next, while nonetheless maintaining links that convey the story.

The interrelatedness of the characters and the plotlines finally becomes apparent as different groups of characters pursue each other across Madrid — Sexi, Riza and Riza's band followed by the Islamicists, who in turn are followed by Queti and Sexi's band Las Ex, and then the empress. The meandering labyrinth straightens out as the central characters come in sight of the happy ending: it is now that Riza connects up the different narrative threads by his explanation to Sexi of why he slept with his stepmother, while Sexi responds with the explanation behind the explanation, that the wicked stepmother was at the root of all their problems. Now that Riza has moved on from the stepmother they can live happily ever after. A chase sequence such as this is typical of comedy films; but the fact that now all follow each other down the same path, their stories now explicitly connected, suggests that we are moving on from the labyrinth. What lies, then, at the end of the complex maze of stories? It is not just the happy ending for the protagonists but also, more prosaically, the airport. At the airport everyone goes their separate ways: their stories break up. The airport is the place that suggests life elsewhere, a place where the characters leave Madrid behind, thus equating Madrid with the labyrinth of confusion, a confusion that is cleared up once the characters leave it.

The crisscrossing of paths will reappear in sequences in *Mujeres al borde de un ataque de nervios*, above all the one in which Pepa emerges to dump Iván's suitcase while Iván is simultaneously trying to phone her: he in turns hides as his mad wife Lucía approaches, while his new lover Paulina, waiting for him in the car, must also hide as Pepa walks past to dump the case. In that case, as we shall see, this crisscrossing — while comical — signifies a lack of communication, people's lack of awareness of each other. The crisscrossing of *Laberinto* does not have quite the same negative connotation, suggesting in this case rather a sense of the complexity and interconnectedness of Madrid and its *movida*. It also suggests the liveliness of life in Madrid and a more literal sense to the notion of the *movida*, or as Brad Epps puts it, that motion implies hysteria, with everybody running around in an unsettled, overly emotional fashion (*17*, p.100).

Homosexuality or heterosexuality?

As we saw in the introduction, over the trajectory of his career Almodóvar has developed a reputation as a gay director, despite his reticence about his private life and — of more concern to us here — the fact that homosexuality does not in fact feature to a large extent in his films. Although many of his films feature characters whose sexuality does diverge from the norm of monogamous and heterosexual behaviour — including transsexual characters — homosexual characters do not feature that greatly, certainly less than we might expect given the director's reputation. *Laberinto* also features gay characters, but whether it is about homosexuality is very much open to debate.

James Mandrell (*8*, p.43) has in his essay on the film remarked on Almodóvar's ambivalence towards gay culture and gay expression in film, as well as his discretion over his own sexuality, and goes on to discuss *Laberinto* in terms of a retreat into heterosexuality, where it is the straight characters who find the happy ending — even Riza, who has given up affairs with men now that he has settled for Sexi (*8*, p.46). This happy ending comes uncomfortably close to the suggestion that homosexuality is curable, if only the man can meet the right woman. As Mandrell remarks: 'the joke of the film is not about those theories of desire that claim homosexuality *as a stage* in the development of the healthy heterosexual but, rather, about homosexuality that claims to be anything *more than a stage* en route to a mature heterosexuality' (*8*, p.53: italics in original). Homosexuality becomes, on this reading, little more than an immature aberration that lies in the ability to break away from one's parents — in this case, Riza's inability to move on from the quasi-incestuous coupling with his stepmother that occurs in one of the flashback sequences. Moreover, homosexuality in *Laberinto* is a desire that is perpetually frustrated in that homosexual acts bring Riza no satisfaction, and they are never perceptible to the audience — both elements in contrast to the loud orgasms of Riza and Sexi in the plane at the end of the film. Homosexuality remains, as Mandrell notes: 'unseeable, unknowable, and, ultimately, inexplicable' (*8*, p.54). This is confirmed when Sexi follows Riza to the guitarist Santi's flat after they first met the night before: both have in the interim had failed sexual encounters because of their lack of interest and enthusiasm. When they meet in Santi's flat, they confess they have not stopped thinking about each other, and immediately they get into bed together. Once this more successful encounter has taken place (although sex does not occur), Riza confesses his true identity as he does not want to lie to her, already putting their relationship on a different footing from his homosexual partners such as Santi and Sadec, to whom he does not reveal who he is. This equation of honesty and the revelation of the real identity with heterosexuality here support the latter as the preferred sexual identity.

Mandrell is right to a certain extent: his reading has force behind it, and the reversion to the heterosexual happy ending does allow us, if we wish, to dismiss homosexuality as part of the local colour that we leave behind at the end of the film, as Riza and Sexi do when they leave Madrid for another country. But the situation is a little more complex than this. Quite how far we should accept Mandrell's reading revolves around the notion of parody. Mandrell himself refers to the film as parody or burlesque, a technique that allows straight audiences a certain amount of distance: the humour means that the film does not in fact threaten the heterosexual norm (*8*, p.53). But the argument rests on the assumption that it is homosexuality that is being parodied: Almodóvar himself, on the other hand, has claimed that the films functions as a parody of teen romance movies with the style of Billy Wilder.[6] Homosexuality itself is, by the very invisibility of it that Mandrell observes, harder to perceive as parody, whereas the search for the happy ending seems more overt a target: the loud orgasms of Riza and Sexi themselves attest to this in their very exaggeration. Almodóvar's references to Wilder reminds us of the American screwball comedy (a notion we will encounter again when we comes to look at *Mujeres al borde de un ataque de nervios*), wherein interrelated plotlines (often labyrinthine like those of *Laberinto*) must be tied up neatly, often with the sense of multiple happy endings. The reversion to the monogamous couple that is typical of such films is what is parodied here, not only with Riza and Sexi's orgasms but the new relationship embarked by Queti, now a clone of Sexi, and Sexi's father, in another heterosexual happy ending that nonetheless looks like incest even if in fact it is not.

There is furthermore a sense of acceptance of homosexuality as unremarkable rather than something that might shock. Sadec's colleagues, for instance, are aware of his homosexuality and do not react beyond a mild irritation that it gets in the way of their mission — though, in the ironically labyrinthine way of the film, it is in fact his homosexuality, combined with his unusual sense of smell, that provides access to the relevant clues and allows their mission to proceed. Homosexuality becomes simply one strand among other forms of sexuality and other forms of relationship interwoven inextricably to form part of the intricate pattern of human life and desire in Madrid. Homosexuality is part of that pattern, no more, no less. Almodóvar has argued for an underlying seriousness within the film concerning how difficult it is for two potential lovers to get together,[7] and the unlikeliness of the happy heterosexual ending merely underscores how difficult the process of finding the object of one's desire actually is, even in the pleasure playground of Madrid.

---

[6] Vidal, p.40.
[7] Vidal, p.40.

Psychoanalysis and incest

For this difficulty there is a scapegoat at hand: sexual trauma induced by the irresponsibility of those who are the elders and, in theory, betters of the central characters. As Mandrell argues (*8*, p.49) the sexual problems of the two protagonists are linked through their shared sexual traumas of childhood that we see in the flashback sequences. Riza's plunge into homosexuality can be seen as a retreat from the possibility of incest with his stepmother, an idea that Mandrell (*8*, p.50) suggests is reinforced when we see Riza pick up Sadec while the stepmother is in a nearby phone box. The threat of incest also affects the young Sexi, causing in turn her nymphomania. These traumas have, in Sexi's case, been subjected to psychoanalysis which by the start of the film has signally failed to find a cure.

Psychoanalysis is rooted in Sigmund Freud's theories of sexual development and the role played by the subconscious in this. According to Freud's theories, incestuous desire lies at the root of all forms of sexuality in adulthood. The little boy sees his mother as his initial object of desire, but the interposition of his father forces him to transfer his desires elsewhere and thus eventually mature into adult heterosexuality: an inability to make this transfer leads to homo-sexual desires. Freud notoriously found it more difficult to account for female sexuality and in particular female same-sex desire, but in a parallel move he posited the desire of the little girl for her father which over time would mutate into a desire to have babies as a substitute for the father's unobtainable penis. This move developed further with the concept of 'penis-envy' — the desire of women to have the penis and thus the power that it symbolises.

Some of the specifics of Freud's theories have since been much disputed; and their validity or otherwise need not concern us here. What does concern us is their basis for psychoanalysis (and popular notions about it), which is also a motif of *Laberinto*. The plot thread of psychoanalysis arises at an early stage in the film, where Sexi discusses with her psychoanalyst Susana her daylight phobia. Here we view the first of the flashback scenes that suggest Sexi's problems lie in her past, her childhood. And only a few minutes later we witness her father commenting to the empress on Sexi's analysis with

Susana, and embedded in this discussion is a clue to part of the problem — the empress herself set in motion the train of events that lead to both Sexi's and Riza's problems: her attempt to seduce her stepson and her dismissal of the young Sexi as a potential rival. This is reinforced with another flashback to the doctor's meeting with the emperor. In the pivotal encounter of Sexi and Riza at the nightclub, Sexi watches Riza perform on stage and is confused by a light shining in her eyes that reminds her of the sun, and immediately Almodóvar inserts a flashback scene to her holiday with her father. Perhaps it is at this point that she mentally substitutes Riza for her father, a transfer of desire that allows her to move on from her nymphomania towards a more mature and exclusive sexual relationship with Riza. Certainly she is in no mood for the group sex which is offered her very soon after her encounter with Riza.

Psychoanalysis is held up to a high level of ridicule in the film. Rather cruelly, Susana's weight — emphasised when she runs desperately after Sexi's father at one point — and her untidy appearance, coupled with her over-obvious attempt to introduce herself to the father the first time they are together, and the subsequent intensity of her futile efforts to seduce him, all combine to make her the butt of humour, and her profession as ridiculous. This serves to imply that psychoanalysis does not ultimately help to supply basic sexual needs and desires, and that people are more likely to be sexually fulfilled if they abandon psychoanalytic treatment: the psychoanalysts themselves experience little pleasure. While Susana is doomed to perpetual frustration, Sexi's father himself has no interest in sex, and his life appears joyless, an idea reflected in the canaries in his office that do not sing (until Queti, disguised as Sexi, drugs them). Susana also demonstrates, however, that the sexual liberation of the *movida* is not for everyone, but apparently confined to the young and stylish rather than the fat and middle-aged. Another tactic Almodóvar uses to undermine psychoanalysis is by giving it melodramatic overtones, as in the conversation between the two mothers in the waiting room, in which one describes her desire to have a child while the other describes her daughter as a burden — all to the accompaniment of excessively romantic violins.

Psychoanalysis is very much bound up with the older generation of characters — Susana and Sexi's father provide the psychoanalysis, while the empress resorts to it as a cure. The fact that psychoanalysis causes the sexual difficulties of Riza and Sexi suggests that their problems also stem from the malign influence of their elders. The central flashback sequence of the film shows us what really happened on the beach that day. As the young Sexi lies buried up to her neck in sand, Riza bores a hole in the sand with his finger, round about where her vagina would be. The scene suggests nascent heterosexual sexuality. But the empress comes along, throws sand spitefully in Sexi's face, wrests Riza away and tries unsuccessfully to seduce him. Sexi, apparently rejected by Riza, and subsequently turned away by her father who is too busy to attend to her, approaches a group of boys on the beach. They ask her to join their game of husbands and wives and she agrees with the significant comment that she will be everyone's wife. This signals the beginning of the promiscuity and group sex that subsequently characterises Sexi's life until she encounters Riza once again and their love for each other gets back on track. Meanwhile Riza rejects the empress: as he watches Sexi about to join in the game of husbands and wives, another boy comes up to him, whispers in his ear, and the two go off together. This implies the beginning of Riza's homosexual career. The attitudes of the parents — indifference from Sexi's father, inappropriate desire from the empress — cause their apparent sexual misalignment. Only by breaking free of the influence of their elders can they sort themselves out.

As we saw in the very brief description of Freud's theories, incestuous desire lies at the heart of infant sexuality. While Brad Epps (*17*, p.105) argues that 'incest, rape and violence are shown to succeed while homosexuality and promiscuity are shown to fail', incest is in fact more problematic than this. Incest provides a major source of trauma in the film, lying as we have seen at the root of the central characters' sexual problems. It also reinforces the sense that hang-ups have been caused by the older generation. It might be stretching it rather far to suggest that the newly liberated youth of the *movida* have dispensed with their sexual repression by repulsing the ideologies of an older generation steeped in the atmosphere of Francoism, so that incest becomes a metaphor for the perverse beliefs of parents and those in authority during the Franco era, which caused such pain and for which the transition to democracy proved such a relief. But it certainly suggests that the inability to freely express sexual desire lies with one's repressed roots: incest is on one level simply being too close to one's parents' generation. Perhaps unintentionally, it also implies that the sexual heterogeneity of the *movida* is in itself no more than a consequence of the inappropriate attitudes of the older generation, and thus a stage to be overcome. As Vidal comments: '*Labyrinth of Passions* is not the most representative of Almodóvar's films, but it was a necessary step for him to move on to newer, more personal ways. Almodóvar had to get modernity out of his system some way, and this was just as good a way as any.'[8]

This does not prevent Almodóvar using the theme of incest for comedy, nor for retaining a trace of it as an alternative means to happiness. This occurs through Queti's story. The disturbing sexual overtures made to her by her father are offset by the humour of her attempts to drug him into quietude (countered by her father's recourse to drugs to improve his libido). She dreams of escape, particularly through her devotion to Sexi and her group (she is to be seen applauding wildly at the end of the band's set). Ironically, she escapes ultimately into another, quasi incestuous relationship with Sexi's father, having agreed with the latter to take her place and having had plastic surgery that ensures her exact resemblance to her idol. Although technically the sexual relationship between Queti and Sexi's father that begins at the end of the film is not incestuous, it functions this way figuratively — Sexi's father believes that Queti is his daughter, while Queti for her part is in a sense a clone of Sexi.

---

[8] Vidal, p.245.

Style

In his previous film *Pepi, Luci, Bom*, Almodóvar had already blazed a stylistic trail of outrage and exaggeration underscored (literally) by a punk sound (with Spanish punk star Alaska appearing in the film as the character Bom). The same is true of *Laberinto*, which lingers for a little at the punk concert in which Almodóvar himself takes part alongside fellow artiste Fabio (or Fanny) McNamara. Although the latter's character carries an important plot function initially in bringing Riza to the punk gig, and thus to meeting Sexi, this is obscured by his function as style statement. More than any other character he is there to suggest outlandishness and excess (to the extent that, as the labyrinthine plot strands become tauter and more closely woven he drops out of sight altogether, just as Riza and Sexi drop their *movida* music in favour of escape together). The opening dialogue of the film centres on Fabio, who sets the tone of the film and gestures towards its roots in *movida* culture. He also suggests the blurring of artistic boundaries in that he both sings and stars in a porn film, just as Almodóvar himself both directs and sings. (Indeed, we witness Almodóvar directing this film, in his most self-referential cameo.) The punk music, however, in its very excess obscures the use of other forms of music that would become more apparent in the director's later films, older forms of music that are a throwback to earlier Spanish popular cultures. For example, the opening credits occur over music reminiscent of the folkloric flamenco films that were popular in the 30s and 40s in Spain. Or when Sexi travels on a train she is accompanied by an older style of music suggesting a fifties thriller. The music can therefore function as another form of kitsch; and perhaps by now, viewing *Laberinto* retrospectively, the punk music itself has become kitsch too.

The film may act as a showcase for the *movida*, but it also moves outside it to offer us scenes of the middle-class and middle-aged, such as the sequences in which Susana's desire for Sexi's father is revealed (including the first flashback shot that prepares us for the more significant beach flashbacks, one of which occurs shortly afterwards). Almodóvar includes many settings of middle-class interiors such as the home and offices of Sexi's father, Susana's

home and the hotel in which Riza meets the empress. Further down
the social scale we also have a short sequence in the *tintorería* of
Queti and her father. These different settings imply that the spirit of
the *movida* is not confined to areas such as the Rastro but percolates
throughout all sectors of Madrid (even if not everybody can
participate). Indeed, a careful analysis of the film suggests that
despite the sense of a caper comedy through the streets of Madrid,
much of the film takes place in small, sometimes claustrophobic
interiors, which adds to the sensation that the excess style cannot be
contained and threatens to overwhelm us: there almost literally is not
any room for it.

Of all the films discussed in this book, *Laberinto* comes closest
to being pure comedy, given its madcap style. As we shall see in
future chapters, however, Almodóvar also has a taste for melodrama
in his films, and even here it reveals itself on occasion, such as the
scene in which Sexi confronts the empress and then runs away to the
accompaniment of dramatic strings. (The empress herself indulges in
some overly melodramatic acting in this scene.) The pivotal flashback scene in which the empress attempts to seduce Riza makes a
similar use of string music. The later attenuation of comedy in films
such as *Todo sobre mi madre* and *Hable con ella* will be associated
with Almodóvar's increasing maturity both in terms of age and of
filmmaking. For now, Almodóvar uses melodrama for the most part
in parodic terms, implied by the use of the thriller music as Sexi rides
on the metro and later as the different groups of characters arrive at
the recording studio in search of Riza, or little melodramatic gestures
such as Sadec's dramatic pause in the airport when he can smell
Riza. In the midst of the *movida*'s excesses, melodrama as excess has
comparatively little prominence.

3. *Matador*

If Almodóvar had continued simply to make films that reflected the *movida*, he would have rapidly become dated, and his films probably no more than a historical curio to tell us of a bygone era. Instead, he began to develop a series of films that would take him closer to the mainstream and earn him the status of the most prominent director of his generation. And in his next films he would develop the trademarks that were to become synonymous with his films — even when, with his later films, he began to diverge from them. At an early stage then, Almodóvar began to favour female characters and plotlines that focused on the emotional desires, and frustrations of women already suggested by *Pepi, Luci, Bom* but less prominent in

Laberinto. *Entre tinieblas* (1983) is overwhelmingly dominated by women, unsurprisingly since the primary setting for a film is a convent. The eccentric collection of nuns (one takes heroin, another writes erotic novels, a third owns a pet tiger) attempt to reach out to the youth of Madrid, so that it subsequently appears as if the world of *Laberinto* has invaded the convent. The use of older forms of music, in particular the bolero, becomes more evident here (see *5*). *¿Qué he hecho yo para merecer esto?* (1984) is a comparatively grim film for Almodóvar, dealing with the struggles of a Madrid housewife, Gloria, simply to get by from day to day, though some of her techniques for doing so, such as selling her son to a paedophile dentist, tap into the zany, amoral universe of the previous films. Almodóvar continues to offer us a kaleidoscope of different sexual desires and practices: lesbianism, prostitution, paedophilia, anonymous sexual encounters, exhibitionism. His characters continue to be comic and eccentric but are no longer confined to the youthful excesses of the *movida*: now they can be found at every age and in every walk of life.

Matador is nonetheless the film that saw Almodóvar's work move closer to the mainstream. And yet *Matador* may seem at first blush an unlikely candidate for such a move, not only because of its violent and sexually explicit opening scene but also its sympathetic portrait of two serial killers. Internationally, *Matador* also offered a subversion of clichés of Spanishness which allowed foreign audiences both to appreciate the subversion while simultaneously indulging in the pleasure of the familiar stereotypes that such subversion inevitably brings to mind. *Matador* also reveals for the first time an intermittent taste on the part of Almodóvar for murder mysteries, even if, as in this case, we know the identity of at least one of the murderers from the beginning. A similar notion is to be found in the director's next film, *La ley del deseo*: while we, the audience, know the identity of the murderers, the other characters do not, and we follow their progress as they solve the mystery. Almodóvar returns to the mystery formula later with *Carne trémula* (itself based on a novel by mystery writer Ruth Rendell), and again with *La mala educación*, though in these later cases we are to begin with as equally in the dark as the characters as to the solution of the mystery. And if *¿Qué he hecho?* suggested the amorality of the working classes, now the director offers us the same elements within middle-class, white-collar society.

The taste for pathological characters

Matador is also the first film in terms of a more particular, if inter-mittent, characteristic of Almodóvar's films and more pronounced in the later films — a sympathetic portrayal of characters whose actions would ordinarily seem beyond the pale. This becomes manifest with the most recent films: in the chapter on *Hable con ella* I will look in more detail at the character of Benigno, an amiable and likeable man who nonetheless is an obsessive stalker who later rapes the comatose object of his desire, leaving her pregnant. *La mala educación* deals with child abuse at school and its consequences: although child abuse is considered a particularly malignant crime, Almodóvar positions the audience viewpoint in such a way that it becomes hard not to share the sorrow of the abuser at the prospective loss of his lover, while his former victim turns out to be unappealing and greedy. Earlier pathological figures include Antonio, the murderous and obsessive lover of Pablo in *La ley del deseo*, who ends the film and his life with a moving encounter with Pablo to the accompaniment of a bolero. In *Carne trémula*, as I shall discuss in my chapter on the film, the secondary character of Sancho appears at first blush to be an unreformed misogynist and wife-beater who engineers the shooting that will disable his colleague and for which an innocent man will be framed. Yet towards the end of the film his vulnerability and his love for his wife makes him a more rounded and less detestable character, even as his desperation to keep his wife leads him to kill first her and then himself.

The first of this series of pathological characters are *Matador*'s central characters Diego (Nacho Martínez) and María (Assumpta Serna), serial killers, and Almodóvar implicitly persuades us to sympathise with them. Both of them prey on their lovers. Diego becomes sexually aroused at the thought of dead women: the opening scene of the film shows him masturbating as he watches film footage of female corpses. He later asks his girlfriend Eva (Eva Cobo) to play dead during a lovemaking session. As the film develops it turns out that some of Diego's female students have vanished, murdered by Diego himself, who has buried them in his garden. María murders her casual lovers with a hairpin in the middle of sex, so that she experiences a solitary climax straddled over a dead body, as we discover in an early sequence.

Put baldly, these do not seem like attractive characters. Yet we come to accept them in all their perversity. Almodóvar achieves this primarily through the all-consuming love affair that develops between the two killers, who recognise in each other kindred spirits. The emotion is further heightened by the fact that their passion can only be fully realised through their simultaneous deaths at the moment of sexual climax. The final sequences in which they spend their last moments together are overtly romantic and sentimental (including the accompanying bolero 'Espérame en el cielo' prior to the film's fatal ending). This ending offers us the pleasure of melodrama. Although there is latent humour in the reaction of the other characters when they arrive late to the scene, it does nothing to detract from Almodóvar's very tongue-in-cheek attitude to romantic drama. The film and its lovers function on one level as a sort of homage to the Hollywood melodramas such as *Duel in the Sun* (King Vidor, 1946), which is playing in the cinema wherein Diego and María first meet face to face. That film, too, tells of an impossible love affair which ends with the lovers killing each other and then embracing one last time, dying in each others' arms. The beauty of this love is acclaimed by the assembled cast of the other characters who act as a sort of Greek chorus commenting on the actions of the gods (and telling us how to think about the events). The sympathy for the lovers thus induced is underscored by the fact that most (though not all) of the events in the film are presented from Diego and/or María's point of view, which is why we know the solution to the mystery of the murders before the other characters do, apart from Ángel (Antonio Banderas).

This seems to ignore the fact that crimes have been committed and victims have died. We learn virtually nothing of the victims, and see only one murder take place. The shock on this victim's face as he is stabbed may well reflect our own surprise, since this death is not part of the scenario we envisage with the sex scene taking place, despite the accompanying voiceover of Diego describing the bullfighting kill. The ambiguous attitude towards the murders is embodied in the police inspector (Eusebio Poncela), who is more eager to prove Ángel innocent than solve the murders (although ironically his attention towards Ángel will in fact lead him to the solution to the crimes). When he arrives at the bullfighting school, he prefers to ogle the crotches of the male bullfighters to asking questions (though again, when he finally does so, we receive clues to the murders). In a similar vein, the attitude toward Ángel suggested by other characters implies in turn a sympathy towards behaviour we might otherwise find unacceptable: the attempted rape of Eva. Almodóvar treats this failed rape in terms of comedy (Ángel bringing out a corkscrew from his pocket rather than a knife with which to threaten Eva). While we might feel uncomfortable with Ángel's actions, the other characters do not. Eva and her mother Pilar (Chus Lampreave) are dismissive of the event, seeing it as no more than an inconvenience, and do not press charges, while the female police officer to whom Ángel first denounces himself remarks that some women have all the luck. In this case Almodóvar leaves us some scope for sympathy by the fact that these events, and his subsequent false claim to the murders, can be perceived as a cry for help, given his oppressive life with his unsympathetic mother (Julieta Serrano), the burden of his visions and the difficulty he may have in coming to terms with his sexuality (although this is left ambiguous).

Gender

Critics have observed in *Matador* a blurring of traditional gender roles between the two central characters so that both share characteristics of masculinity and femininity regardless of biological sex. This might seem initially surprisingly, since María functions as a *femme fatale* (see *10*), while Diego is a bullfighter — figures of overt and predatory female sexuality and masculine strength and prowess. Things are, however, not that simple. María blurs the gender boundaries through her work as a lawyer (a traditionally masculine occupation), and the business suit of strident black and white checks which she wears throughout much of the film. When she is not wearing business suits, she dresses in the guise of a matador, as at the fashion show and subsequently when she wraps herself up in the bullfighter's cape that Diego gives her as a gift — again, clothing that suggests the traditionally masculine profession of bullfighting rather than the feminine.

In fact the *femme fatale* is more problematic than the stereotype of sultry siren might suggest. Mary Ann Doane in her discussion of the *femme fatale* draws on the concept of femininity as masquerade as originally posited by Joan Riviere in her essay 'Womanliness as Masquerade'.[9] Riviere argues that women use overt femininity as a masquerade to cover up their real intentions of moving around and surviving in a male-dominated world, and more particularly to disguise an intent to lay claim to masculine power.[10] In some ways the *femme fatale*'s overt feminine sexuality — feared and yet desired by men — is what a more traditional femininity might be thought to mask, a devouring and dangerous sexuality and a desire to oust man from his place of power. But, as Doane has it, the *femme fatale* is not so much the truth about women laid bare but a site of 'discursive unease'. She argues:

> The seductive power attributed to the figure of the *femme fatale* in film noir exemplifies the disparity between seeming and being, the deception, instability, and unpredictability associated with the woman. While the organization of vision in the cinema pivots around the representation of the woman — she is always aligned with the quality of to-be-looked-at-ness — it is also the case that in her attraction to the male subject she

[9] Mary Ann Doane, *Femmes Fatales: Feminism, Film, Psychoanalysis* (New York: Routledge, 1991), pp. 33–34.

[10] Riviere is also at pains to point out, however, that we cannot distinguish the masquerade of femininity from an authentic female identity or, as Riviere puts it, 'womanliness', that lies behind it.

confounds the relation between the visible and the knowable.[11]

To put it more simply, we cannot trust the image of the woman that we see on the screen to give us an accurate indication of what her nature might be. As María herself says to Diego when he points out that she should not be in the men's lavatory, one should not trust appearances ('No te fíes de las apariencias'): we cannot automatically pigeonhole her on the grounds of overt gender differences. But if María confounds the relation between the visible and the knowable of gender, then so does Diego. Bullfighting, and the matador in particular, have an ambivalent relation to issues of gender. Almodóvar has himself commented on the feminine aspects of the matador, who 'teases and seduces' the bull in the early stages of the *corrida*: his balletic movements and tight costume are not entirely masculine.[12] Teasing and seducing, too, are terms more automatically aligned with the feminine rather than the masculine: the whole process could be regarded as a feminine tease. The matador also possesses, in Doane's phrase, the 'quality of to-be-looked-at-ness': the suit of lights that the matador wears is ornate, reminiscent of the glamorous costumes worn by many a *femme fatale*. We could argue, too, that his accident in the ring has emasculated him (an idea underscored by his lameness). So if María lays claim to the masculine, Diego also lays claim to the feminine. They blur traditional gender boundaries, and recognise that they do so: when María comments that all murderesses have something of the masculine in them, Diego replies by saying that all murderers have something of the feminine. This blurring of the boundaries is thus transgressive, tied up with murder. This move does not mean that Almodóvar is implicitly condemning a move away from defined gender roles, given the sympathy he elicits for the couple, but it does suggest the questioning of heterosexual desire taken to its extreme, in contrast to the heterosexual reconciliation of Sexi and Riza in *Laberinto*. Smith (*14*, p.187) comments: 'The moral of *Matador* is

---

[11] Doane, p.46.
[12] Frederic Strauss, *Almodóvar On Almodóvar* (London: Faber, 1994), p.57.

that there is no sexual relation: heterosexuals can achieve reciprocity only when sexual difference itself is suspended in fantasy or death.' If in *Laberinto* the heterosexual happy ending proved facile, here it proves impossible, since both characters die at the moment of climax. If there is heterosexual union the characters are not alive to experience it. Gender is blurred but not united.

The parallel sequences at the beginning of the film that intercut Diego's bullfighting class with shots of María murdering her sexual partner echo the parallel nature of the double masquerade: María has clearly learnt well the lesson on how to be a good matador. Smith (*3*, p.6) has noted the confusion and discontinuity to which this particular cross-cutting sequence gives rise. We are reminded of the semantic unease contained within the word 'matador'. In terms of the sphere of stereotyped images and ideas of Spain, the word in Spanish carries an aura of vibrant if controversial Spanish spectacle, related as it is to the bullfight, but elsewhere it simply means 'killer', and the parallel sequences stress this idea. María plays on this dual meaning when she confesses to Diego that she did not approach him before because she did not realise that he was still a matador. The parallel sequences suggest the impossibility of distinguishing between the two meanings — an unease that becomes more blatant as we come to realise that Diego is a killer of women as well as a matador retired from the ring. These confusions over meanings again relate to Doane's ideas over the confusion and unease that masquerade inspires. The matador is, of course, clearly marked out as a site of spectacle of Spanishness, the object of everyone's gaze: his whole *raison d'être* revolves around his role as the object of spectacle in a very visual Spanish ritual — a ritual aimed at sight above all other senses. But María lays claim to this, too: her method of murder mimics that of the matador, at one point she dresses in a swirling cape much like that of the matador (and she also persuades Diego to give her his old bullfighting cape as a memento), and she collects souvenirs of Diego's past career in the ring, putting them on display to provide a fetishistic spectacle for her eyes alone. Marvin D'Lugo comments that 'the stereotypical bullring image of Spanish cultural space is transformed into a space of seduction in which the female, not the male, is predator' (*4*, p.136).

Leora Lev argues that despite the blurring of gender boundaries, María can only acquire masculine empowerment by becoming a clone of Diego, so that in consequence '[e]rasure of inequality seems necessarily to imply occultation of feminine difference' (*13*, p.82). But as we have seen, the matador himself blurs the boundaries between male and female and functions many times over as a site of discursive unease. As María comes to align herself with the role of the matador in both senses of the word, she confuses things still further: she does not so much attempt to usurp the male role as recognise its ambiguities that find an echo in her own position. As Barry Jordan and Rikki Morgan-Tamosunas suggest, the two killers reject 'gender binaries as they recognise one another as members of the same species, beyond gender difference'.[13] What María does appear to usurp is the sense of spectacle: by mimicking the bullfighter she participates subversively in the ritual of the bullfight and thus in this ritual of Spanish masquerade.

Nation and stereotype

Until very recently, *Matador* was the only work where Almodóvar tackled head on the more overt clichés of Spanishness, and above all bullfighting. Bullfighting has reappeared in his later film *Hable con ella*, but the later film is not 'about' bullfighting in the way that *Matador* is: bullfighting in *Hable con ella* serves primarily as an easy device with which to place a character in a coma. Smith (*3*, p.74) points out that *Matador* was a more successful film in Spain than other iconic representations of Spanishness such as the flamenco of respected art director Carlos Saura's *El amor brujo*, which received more funding than *Matador* but which, unlike the latter, gave a negative return. Smith argues that *Matador* 'struck something of a chord with Spanish audiences at a particular historical moment, when other films on national themes […] did not' (*3*, p.74). He points to a

---

[13] Barry Jordan and Rikki Morgan-Tamasounas, *Contemporary Spanish Cinema* (Manchester: Manchester University Press, 1998), p.152.

revival of interest in bullfighting at this time; and distinguishes foreign critiques of the film that saw it as a reconfirmation of a national trope, and Spanish critique which perceived it as 'the reworking of a cultural tradition that carried within it, necessarily, a certain social history' (*3*, p.75). But there is arguably a negative side to this use of familiar national images. While the director might treat these images playfully, serving not only to insert them as still valid images in contemporary cinema but to subvert them as well (reminding us, too, of the dual meaning of the very word 'matador'), there remains the danger that the viewer might simply take the images at face value as simple truths about Spanish culture while neglecting the possibility of subversion. We are reminded of Barry Jordan's comments, quoted in the introduction, of the potential to pander to a stereotype of Spain as death and (now perverse) passion. The subversion of these stereotypes, however, occurs with a reflection on Almodóvar's growing tendency to draw on a ragbag of cultural styles and artefacts that occurred in earlier films and would occur again in later films. Just as he had begun to recycle older forms of Hispanic music, so the familiar tropes of Spanishness can be recycled. But their timelessness is also subverted in their application to contemporary Spanish society and its transformation of gender roles.

A more overt parody of Spanish culture, albeit a passing reference, comes with the fashion designer's remark about his show as 'Spain divided', drawing on the deep historical and cultural rift between conservative and liberal Spain that ultimately gave rise to the Spanish Civil War and the Franco regime. Smith (*3*, p.75) and Lev (*13*, p.80) both discuss the fashion show as an opportunity for a Spanish spectator to rethink what it means to be Spanish. As Smith observes, the designer's use of the term reveals 'a playful register which deprives such clichés of their continuing relevance' (*3,* p.75). The division of Spain into two is reflected in the characters of the two mothers of the film (as in *Laberinto* the older generation stand as markers of Spain's past). Ángel's mother (Julieta Serrano), a member of Opus Dei, and cold and religiously fanatic to the point of despising her sensitive son as irredeemable, represents the conservative, Francoist past. Eva's mother Pilar, however, is forward-looking and fashionable, dressing in cheerful colours, devoted to her daughter, sympathetic and fun. Both are caricatured to some extent, perhaps hinting at the fact that the notion of the Spanish divide is itself overly simplistic a way to understand Spanish culture. There can, however, be little doubt in this film, at least, as to which side of this divide our sympathies should lie, given the embodiment of the two sides of the divide in the two very different mothers. Ángel's mother, indeed, suggests how older traditions continue to stifle and stunt some of Spain's children. But the concept of the two Spains is diminished in importance by its very reduction to a fashion motif, part of the cultural bricolage of which Almodóvar's films partake.

Death and ritual

Mark Allinson (*1*, p.27) prefaces his discussion of death and desire in *Matador* with observations concerning the centrality of death to Spanish culture. In modification of this equation between death and Spanish culture he refers to Georges Bataille, who believed that all human sexuality is 'irrational, excessive and even murderous, qualities which depend not on historical or geographical-cultural contexts, but on a timeless need for taboos and for their transgression' (*1*, p.30), so that the national context may not matter so much. Nonetheless, while sexuality may not be dependent on a specific national context, it can be expressed through it. Both Diego and María's desire for death plays itself out through the bullfight — Diego who cannot renounce the thrill of the final kill, and María's use of her hairpin in imitation of the bullfighter. This linking of death to this Spanish motif reaches its height in the final scene, as the lovers die lying on top of bullfighting capes.

According to Allinson (*1*, p.27), *Matador* is the only film of Almodóvar to explore the relation between death and desire. This close relationship is posited from the very beginning of the film as Diego masturbates to video clips of dead women; and we are reminded of it in the passionate encounter between Diego and María on the Segovia viaduct, a well-known suicide spot in Madrid. More cruelly, we are reminded of it in Diego's insistence to Eva that she play dead when they make love. This line of thought is also maintained more tenuously — and more comically — in the opportunity taken by the police inspector to look at the crotches of the bullfighters as they are practising their death thrusts, just before approaching them to ask questions about their missing colleagues. Does he also take pleasure in their rehearsal for death? The threat of death can also be turned into a fashion statement, as when the fashion designer (a delightful cameo by Almodóvar himself) insists on highlighting the scar that Eva received in the course of her failed rape by Ángel (and thus deriving from a perverse expression of desire), and gives her a gun to hide in her costume. She is modelling an avant-garde wedding dress for a mock marriage with a man symbolising Death. The lighter moments serve to parody even the seriousness of the link between death and desire, so that although we get caught up in the passion between Diego and María a subversive note of parody intermittently reminds us that even in this relationship the director may be recycling the tradition of death with his tongue firmly in his cheek.

Bullfighting can be perceived on one level as a form of ritual sacrifice in which, on the whole, the outcome is preordained (accidents such as Diego's injury notwithstanding). Dominic Keown (*12*, p.346) suggests that although Almodóvar encourages us to take the spectacle of the film at face value, there nonetheless exists a subtext that relates the bull to pagan fertility rites and symbols, as suggested by the circle motif that appears intermittently throughout the film (the bullrings, diagrams, Eva's earrings), suggestive of ritual sites. María's devotion to Diego's former career as bullfighter — her collection of memorabilia forming a veritable shrine to him — is reminiscent of a priestly attitude: her pursuit of a similar murderous career to his, using his techniques, suggests the attitude of an acolyte. Diego and María also come complete with their own mystic who can interpret their actions to outsiders, and who has visions of them: Ángel. The eclipse at the end of the film, which occurs just at the moment of Diego and María's fateful climax, is also a wondrous event with primitive religious significance.[14] It is notable that the other characters, hurrying to the final scene, pause for a moment to view the eclipse and in so doing arrive too late to intervene and prevent the deaths, a suggestion of fate, events beyond human control. As Julia says in response to Ángel's lament that he could not save Diego, nobody could save him. He was fated to die. Almodóvar himself comments that 'the metaphor in the movie is the eclipse, the idea of two stars that are interposed but in this new convergence, they begin to glow even more brightly and intensely'.[15]

Religious ritual appears fairly frequently in Almodóvar's work: it offers opportunities for kitsch spectacle, as in Tina and Ada's altar (complete with icons such as a plaster statuette of Marilyn Monroe) in *La ley del deseo* or a moment of self-realisation, as in the tender wedding ceremony attended by Marco and Lydia in *Hable con ella*. Almodóvar uses ritual to tell us of the innermost desires of the characters, and clearly this is true of *Matador* as well. While Almodóvar offers critique of abusive priests, as found in *La ley del deseo* and *La mala educación*, a critique also found here in the oppressive dedication to Catholicism of Ángel's mother, his films do not express a blanket condemnation of the religious and the spiritual. Instead, ritual provides an opportunity for the blending of spiritual and physical desire. Thus the ritual that is Diego and María's pursuit of death and desire is the expression of their innermost being that culminates in the ecstasy of their final encounter, as observed by the police inspector on seeing their bodies. The elements come together in the song 'Espérame en el cielo' that plays on the soundtrack as Diego and María make love: since the song cuts out when we cut to the pursuers in their car, this raises the possibility that the song is diegetic, played by Diego and María themselves to celebrate their final moments. The song celebrates both love and death in its suggestion of an afterlife, but it is also another example of kitsch recycling.

---

[14] Vidal, p.260.
[15] Vidal, p.138.

Voyeurism and identification

Death on screen always carries with it an element of voyeurism, and Smith has pointed to voyeurism as an explicit element of death in *Matador* (*3*, p.67). Again, this is very apparent from the opening scene when Diego masturbates to the necrophilic images on the television, and the police inspector looking at the crotches of the bullfighting students from behind a bush. The ultimate voyeur of the film is, however, Ángel by means of his clairvoyance. He 'witnesses' the murders and thus can tell the police with the bodies of Diego's victims are buried. He is also able to guide the party in pursuit of the lovers to their final meeting place, and on the way he relays Diego and María's actions and dialogue, thus as acting as voyeur of their final sexual encounter. Ángel is a voyeur in a more familiar sense as well, spying on his neighbour Eva in the shower, but voyeurism can imply powerlessness (watching rather than acting), and this is confirmed with Ángel's failed rape (exemplified by his clumsy management of the Swiss army knife that should be a threatening weapon).

The character of Ángel gives a saintly touch to the question of voyeurism. His visions, as observed above, give him the status of a virtual mystic, who can interpret the actions of his gods to mere mortals. This notion is underscored by his innocence: the fact that he is patently not guilty of the crimes to which he confesses, the fact that he faints at the sight of blood, and the fact that he needs mothering (which he eventually receives from the psychiatrist Julia, played by Carmen Maura). We might even add to this list the martyrdom he suffers at the hands of his mother. His name, of course, also implies a saintly quality. This should not, however, obscure the issue of identification that Ángel raises for us the audience. Ángel identifies with Diego, and confesses to Diego's crimes partly to protect him. When he reveals the locations of the bodies to the police, he apologises to Diego for the attempted rape of Eva and obliquely for giving him away, saying that Diego can trust him. He pursues Eva primarily because she is Diego's girlfriend, and his sympathy for the lovers Diego and María facilitates his vision of their final moments. He is on their side. And this raises the question for us the audience:

are we on their side, too? With whom do we identify in the film, if anybody? To identify as an audience with the lovers does not automatically mean that we share a taste for serial murder, but Almodóvar, as I mentioned above, weights the film in favour of our hope for, and vicarious participation in, the realisation of Diego and María's transcendent desire. Thus we are like Ángel, and Ángel's saintly status also sanctifies and excuses us as we participate in a similar sort of voyeurism ourselves. And like Ángel, we have the foreknowledge that he has of the guilty party: we see María's murder of her victim, Diego's masturbation to his videoclips, and the mutual confession of their guilt. We are witnesses to their love in the same way he is. The power of the narrative means that we ourselves may also take pleasure at one remove in the murders that bring the lovers together, resulting in a story of passion. The pleasure may not be the masturbatory pleasure of Diego, but it is nonetheless hard to exempt ourselves from participation in the blend of death and desire that Almodóvar offers to us.

Style

Although Almodóvar's cinema was always considered colourful in the looser sense of his zany, comic style with an emphasis on spectacle, *Matador* is nonetheless the first film in which colour begins to play a more prominent role (see *1*, pp.182–83). Given the plot and major themes of the film, it comes as no surprise that they are supported in terms of colour by a frequent use of red, the colour associated with blood, danger and passion. It is also associated in *Matador* with women, most obviously María and the attention drawn on more than one occasion to her red lipstick (as she looks at herself in the rear view mirror, and as she interviews Ángel for the first time, when only her red mouth is visible). Her surname, Cardenal, also means red. Eva, too, wears red: the avant garde wedding dress in which the mock marriage with Death is staged. Eva dons the dress later when she goes to plead with Diego not to leave her, and overhears his confession of guilt to María. Both María and Diego are bathed in red light as they watch the final scene of *Duel in the Sun*, while the final moments of the film are also bathed in red light, as the camera comes to focus finally on the bodies of the dead lovers, covered in red rose petals. Since *Duel in the Sun* prefigures the romantic but deadly ending of *Matador*, the red colour provides a match and thus a further link to the two scenes. The result is that *Matador* has a rich and vibrant appearance, saturated by the colour red but with other occasional notes of bright colour such as the red and yellow costume that María wears to the fashion show, Diego's pink bullfighting cape and the pink suit of Eva's mother Pilar.

There is also an emphasis in the film on fashion, though this is not the innovation that colour is, as attention is drawn to fashion in *Laberinto de pasiones*. The most obvious locus for fashion in *Matador* is, of course, the fashion show. Marvin D'Lugo writes rather disparagingly of this sequence as the reduction of Spain's 'ideological conflict to a fashion show' (*4*, p. 135). Smith sees the sequence as illustrating fashion as 'a modernity which participates in psychic rather than historic realities' (*3*, p. 75). As we have observed in discussing the question of nation, the sequence grants Spanish spectators an opportunity to perceive their own Spanishness in new ways, as old binary interpretations of reality are parodied and blurred. But confining discussion of this sequence to its link to Spanish history neglects the fact that the fashion show is part of a continuum throughout the film that takes fashion and its glamour and spectacle beyond the confines of the catwalk into everyday life. This is indicated when María, in a dramatic red and yellow costume topped with a black cape (reminding us of the bullfight once more) flees the fashion show into the streets of Madrid, with Diego in pursuit. This movement is echoed when Eva wears her red dress later in pursuit of Diego. Almodóvar also sends up fashion, not only in the exaggerated intensity of the designer but in the overly bright pink suit of Eva's mother Pilar. Although Pilar might appear slightly ridiculous in the suit, she nonetheless has her revenge in the parody of the model's walk and pose as she leaves her daughter in the dressing room, crosses the catwalk and goes to find her seat. But fashion can have more sinister purposes, too, as with María's elaborate hair pin that functions as a murder weapon.

Apart from the use of the closing song, already mentioned above, much of the soundtrack incorporates melancholy or dramatic strings or piano. When María is dressed in her bullfighting style, the music changes to a slow guitar theme, underscoring the link to national stereotypes: Diego also chases her through a dance to the accompaniment of traditional Spanish tunes, in particular the well-known 'Cielito lindo'. The director's use of music points up the fact that *Matador*, particularly towards its end, reveals the director's sense of melodrama, in contrast to the more overt comedy of *Laberinto*. Melodrama is a term that originally referred to drama with song, and that meaning recurs intermittently in Almodóvar's work: we find it here, with the final song as the lovers take their last embrace, and we shall also examples in the next film under discussion, *Mujeres al borde de un ataque de nervios*, and the later *Carne trémula*. But nowadays we take melodrama to be the use of heightened, even exaggerated, emotion that is usually to do with either romance or family love. This emotion is often unrequited or self-sacrificial. The use of melodrama had already become apparent with the earlier *Entre tinieblas*, which ends as the Mother Superior realizes that Yolanda, the object of her love, has abandoned her. In *Matador*, too, we have exaggerated passion to the extent of being deadly, that is also sacrificial and perhaps even unrequited (since the moment they consummate their desire, they cannot be aware of it as they die at that moment). This ending inspires the melodramatic comments of the other characters. Incidental music is often also melodramatic, sometimes to the extent of verging on parody, as in the string music (with thunder) that matches Ángel's attempted rape, or the sound of a harp as Diego catches sight of María disappearing into mist (which is actually exhaust fumes). The stronger emphasis on melodrama does not nonetheless mean an absence of comic touches, such as the fashion show, the police inspector's voyeurism, and a few amusing one-liners; but they function as grace notes compared to the overt comedy of *Laberinto*. Almodóvar repeats this formula in his next film, *La ley del deseo*. It was in the film after *La ley* that Almodóvar formulated a happy mixture of melodrama and comedy: *Mujeres al borde de un ataque de nervios*.

4. *Mujeres al borde de un ataque de nervios*

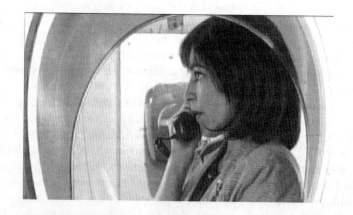

Matador and the film that followed it, *La ley del deseo* (1987), were films of dark passion that ended murderously. The film that came after these two, *Mujeres al borde de un ataque de nervios* (1988), differs in having no murder and no scenes of explicit sex. Whereas the previous two films could be understood in terms of melodrama with comic moments, *Mujeres* is a more thoroughgoing comedy, although moments of melodrama have not been abandoned. *Mujeres*, as its title clearly implies, is centred very heavily on the female characters. As I have already observed, Almodóvar has acquired a reputation as a woman's director, making films focusing primarily on women, sympathetic to women and considering their concerns rather than those of men. This reputation has been nuanced more recently with *Hable con ella* and *La mala educación*, films in which male romantic desires are stressed and in which women have little or nothing to say (as we will discover in the chapter on *Hable con ella*).

By the time of *Mujeres*, however, Almodóvar had gathered round him a group of actresses who appeared repeatedly in his films, above all Carmen Maura[16] but also Chus Lampreave and Rossy de Palma who would both appear in subsequent films. Later additions to the group would include Marisa Paredes, Victoria Abril and Penélope Cruz, who would become the best-known actress of this group given her success in Hollywood as well as Spanish cinema. This group, dubbed the *chicas Almodóvar*, acted as the director's female entourage, boosting his reputation as sympathetic towards women. But *Mujeres* has also contributed greatly to this reputation, being a film in which women appear to triumph unaided by men, who are for the most part the villains of the piece.

Mujeres is not a totally new departure for Almodóvar, as some trademarks persist, including the moments of comedy, emphasis on women's fashions, colour (which first came to prominence in *Matador*), and use of specifically Hispanic songs. But in many ways the mixture of Almodovarian elements in *Mujeres* is more easily digestible to mainstream audiences, lacking as it does those motifs, such as the combination of sexual satisfaction and murder that characterised *Matador*, that might be more controversial. Although *Mujeres* is not without its problems in terms of underlying ideologies, it is on the surface a more easily acceptable comedy that amuses but does not offend. Thus it is not surprising that this is the film that gave Almodóvar real prominence internationally as well as being a domestic success, because of its accessibility. The film was also the Spanish selection for the Best Foreign Film at the Oscars for the relevant year, which suggests that the Spanish film establishment, which had hitherto held Almodóvar somewhat at arms' length, were now more reconciled to his growing prominence and success in Spanish cinema — or at least, they thought *Mujeres* stood the best chance of success, indicating clear eyes if not rosy ones on their part.

---

[16] At the Oscar ceremony for which *Mujeres* was nominated, Maura and Almodóvar famously had a row which produced a deep rift between the two, and for a long time Maura did not appear in any more of the director's films. But after a gap of nearly two decades he directed her in his film *Volver*.

The film makes overt allusions to Hollywood films, and primarily to the romantic comedies and woman-centred melodramas of the 1950s. The clearest example is the Western melodrama *Johnny Guitar* (Nicholas Ray, 1954), with Joan Crawford and Sterling Hayden, dubbed in the film by Pepa and Iván. There are also references to *How to Marry a Millionaire* (Jean Negulesco, 1953), with the women-centred flat and the city backdrop, and to Alfred Hitchcock's *Rear Window* (1954) in the scene where Pepa watches the activities going in different flats within Lucía's apartment block, including a scene of a woman dancing in her underwear, replicating sequences from Hitchcock's film. (For a more detailed listing of Hollywood references, see *18*.) Although many of Almodóvar's films make nods to Hollywood genres, *Mujeres,* with its use of urbane screwball comedy, and middle-class setting, is more reminiscent of Hollywood than most. Barry Jordan argues that *Mujeres* functions basically as an American comedy shot in Spain, so it is hard to describe it as a specifically Spanish film.[17] This raises questions as to how Spain is actually represented in Almodóvar's work as well as to the definition of what is a specifically Spanish film. The lack of Spanish specificity of *Mujeres* may have helped in making the film more digestible for non-Spanish audiences and thus contributed to its international success.

Women

The film's plot follows the efforts of Pepa (Carmen Maura) to sort out the emotional problems from which she is suffering: her break-up with, and her need for and simultaneously her anger with, the father of her forthcoming child, Iván (Fernando Guillén). At the same time she gives help to her friend Candela (María Barranco), another woman in need of support after a traumatic break-up (with a Shi'ite terrorist). The other most prominent character, Lucía (Julieta Serrano), has become slightly deranged after her own break-up with her husband — Pepa's lover Iván. These three break-ups form the motor of the whole film, and also give rise to the plot: the nervous

---

[17] Jordan, p.74.

breakdowns refer to the trauma each woman suffers as a result of the split with her partner.

In some ways *Mujeres* is more affirming of women, than, say, the powerful but murderous María of *Matador*. The women of *Mujeres* are more immediately likeable and sympathetic. While this is obvious of the central character Pepa and the ditzy Candela, it is also true of Lucía, who comes across initially as a ridiculous figure, but also eventually somebody to be pitied. It is hard not to feel sorry for her when, arrested by police for trying to shoot Iván (itself an act suggesting her pain rather than anything darker), she tells the police to take her to the insane asylum, for that is where she belongs. Evans (*18*, p.47) observes an equation between home and the madhouse, when Lucía refers to the latter at the end as home. Both home and asylum have been traps for her, implying a critique of traditional female roles. Another initially unpleasant character, Marisa (Rossy de Palma), becomes softer and more thoughtful after her sexual dream, insisting that Pepa rather than herself should be seated comfortably because of her pregnancy. *Mujeres* suggests the importance of female solidarity: the one unsympathetic female character, Paulina (Kiti Manver), is one who refuses to help her sisters in distress (ironically, being a feminist). Almodóvar also distinguishes the women from the men by the fact that it is the latter who are the root of the women's problems, while women are the ones who come up with solutions. In many cases this means rejecting men altogether. Despite the fact that she spends most of the film trying to talk to Iván, Pepa finally rejects him even after he belatedly offers to reconcile (an empty and melodramatic gesture on his part after she has saved his life). She ends the film talking to another woman instead (Marisa). She finally decides to have her baby without help from its father. Thus from being dependent on Iván Pepa moves to take charge of her own destiny and becomes stronger. Marisa, too, learns to do without men, and this indicates a positive change in her, as she stops domineering her fiancé Carlos (Antonio Banderas) and acts in a more pleasant and open way. This comes about as a result of her solitary orgasm, self-induced through her dream without the assistance of any actual man (the content of her dream is not revealed to us). This virginal orgasm indicates that a man is not essential to achieving sexual pleasure. In this discussion of positive women it is important to give due credit to those very *chicas Almodóvar* who embody these roles, above all Carmen Maura in the pivotal role of Pepa, with a track record of playing strong women or those who overcome bad odds (such as her role in Almodóvar's *¿Qué he hecho yo para merecer esto?*). The strong performances of the actresses reinforce the positive attitude we are encouraged to adopt towards the female characters.

However, the attitude towards women of *Mujeres* is not totally benign. Women are also objects of pathos and ridicule. If we consider Lucía again, we can perceive that sympathy for her plight is not the only reaction Almodóvar attempts to instil in us. Lucía is the butt of much of the film's comedy: we laugh at her rather than with her. The most overt form of comedy is her outlandish and dated clothing (notably the leopard skin hat in which we first see her). She dresses in this way to please her father, and thus she becomes an object of ridicule to make others happy rather than herself. It is notable that it is a man she attempts to please, since her mother is critical both of Lucía's dress code and her attitude towards her father. Lucía appears comic, if also more menacing, in the later chase to the airport. With her hair streaming back in the wind as she rides on the motorbike (to the accompaniment of a thumping trombone music that underscores the humour of her appearance) and later, as she rides the escalators, her hair dishevelled, she looks mad, monstrous (reminiscent of the Medusa) but also comic. The prevention of her final mad act against Iván serves further to humiliate her: she is knocked over by an airport trolley (pushed in her direction by Pepa); and as she rolls to the ground she reveals her underwear, which serves to humiliate her still further.

Lucía is not alone in receiving such negative treatment. Candela's frantic attitude is equally an opportunity for laughter, as she runs desperately around her room in panic at the news report on Shi'ite terrorism and struggles across a rubbish tip to dispose of the evidence of her relationship with the terrorist, or as she is bodily hauled over Pepa's balcony after trying to throw herself off it. (The latter incident provides an opportunity for Iván's son Carlos to put his hand on her bottom, which tells us something about Carlos's own attitudes to women but also suggests that Candela's desperation does not protect her from being seen as a sex object.) The most unpleasant character of all, Paulina, becomes humorous because of the contrast between her treatment of women and her avowed feminism, which suggests that women may be more sympathetic if they avoid what might seem the stridency of actually fighting for one's rights. Even minor characters come in for negative humour: while the religious beliefs of the concierge may offer more benign humour, it is harder to say this for the shrill, painful voice of the telephone operator.

A particular question of relevance here is that of hysteria, the women on the verge of an all too familiar nervous breakdown. Hysteria is a disease inherently associated with women (although recently scholars such as Elaine Showalter[18] have also begun to look at male hysteria, suggesting that women do not have the monopoly on the condition, although when men suffer from it it tends to be called by another name). Labelling women as hysterical is both a technique to render them dangerous and thus in need of control by men, but also to dismiss their emotional demands. G. S. Rousseau remarks:

> [...] hysteria, at least until the early nineteenth century, has been so inextricably entwined with the lot of women that the two can hardly be separated. Unquenchable sexual appetite was long thought to lie at the very root of the malady [...] And the noteworthy aspect of this voracious female desire [...] is that besides being inherently contagious it was conceptualized as *morally dangerous*.[19]

---

[18] Elaine Showalter, *Hystories: Hysterical Epidemics and Modern Culture* (London: Picador, 1998).

[19] G.S. Rousseau, '"A Strange Pathology": Hysteria in the Early Modern World, 1500–1800', in *Hysteria Beyond Freud*, eds Sander Gilman et al (Berkeley: University of California Press, 1993), 91–221 (p.105).

These ideas continue to persist since the nineteenth century, and clearly present hysterical women as a problem that needs to be solved. Medical discourse until very recently perceived hysteria as a manifestation of unfulfilled sexual desire. On this interpretation, women needed sexual satisfaction — a man — to cure them. This would mean marriage in the view of most medical theorists (since, again until recently, marriage was the only socially acceptable way for women to gain sexual satisfaction). This emphasis increased with the advent of psychoanalysis, particularly Freud and Breuer and their classic *Studies on Hysteria* (and we might like to bear in mind Almodóvar's parody of psychoanalysis in *Laberinto de pasiones*). Hysteria as a feminine characteristic also stands opposed to male qualities of rational thinking. It can thus be used as a mechanism with which to attempt to keep women under control.

Brad Epps has written about the motif of hysteria in Almodóvar's films:

> in Almodóvar's production of nervous, rattled women; in
> his depiction of passion, obsession, and repression; and
> in his self-reflective play with voice, body, image, and
> movement there lies, I believe, the historical residue of
> hysteria […]. (*17*, p.101)

And Epps describes *Mujeres* as an example of 'keeping women hysterically on the move' (p.108). Hysteria suggests that women's traumas lie in the lack of a man; and certain elements of the film contradict the progress made by Pepa as she frees herself from male control. While Pepa and Lucía are better off without men, Candela still appears to be dependent on them, having transferred her affection to Carlos. Marisa may achieve orgasm independently of a man but she still needs sexual satisfaction to make her more sympathetic (Pepa notes of the changed Marisa that she has lost that hard look that virgins have, suggesting Marisa as no longer a virgin but also that virgins never look acceptable.) There is also a parallel between Pepa and the film she dubs, *Johnny Guitar*, in which the heroine Vienna (Joan Crawford) may be strong, running her own business, but she still needs a man to help and save her, and to make her life complete. Without men, then, women come apart — literally, if we think of the opening credit sequence, featuring a selection of female body parts, dressed in feminine fashion but suggesting at the same time women's literal breakdown. Elisabetta Girelli (*19*, p.254) reads this opening sequence rather differently, as a hint at the construction and masquerade of femininity foregrounded in the rest of the film (and in her article): the motif of masquerade is repeated from its use in *Matador* and again indicates the impossibility of distinguishing a real woman from a performance of femininity. This concept of the masquerade suggests the absence, the lack of identity and solidity, at the heart of female nature which returns us once more to the idea of women as unstable.

Epps describes the realisation that women can survive without men as 'a sort of bedraggled feminist triumph' (*17*, p.116), and this chimes in with what we have considered here, the downside of the film's portrayal of women. When Gwynne Edwards, then, wonders why critics can perceive the film as hostile to women — 'How anyone can accuse Almodóvar of misogyny remains a mystery'[20] — he is only telling us part of the story. The position of the women in the film certainly does not require the traditional pairing off of many romantic comedies to ensure a happy ending (though even here Pepa attempts something of the sort at the end, allotting the telephone repair man to Marisa now that Carlos has paired off with Candela). But compromise is nonetheless required in order to disentangle the complications of the women's lives and move on, as is surprisingly realistic given the parodic nature of Almodóvar's comedy.

Men

To swing the gender pendulum in another direction, we can also observe that this is also a film very critical of traditional male gender roles, seeing them at the root of all the problems the women experience. If there are negative elements to the depiction of the

---

[20] Gwynne Edwards, *Almodóvar: Labyrinths of Passion* (London: Peter Owen, 2001), p.97.

women, then there is very little positive to say about Iván and to a
lesser extent Carlos. Peter Evans (*18*, p. 40) remarks: 'while the film
recognises that masculinity is in crisis, it never doubts the
responsibility not just of Iván but of the patriarchal order as a whole
for leading women to the brink of mental collapse.' And for this Iván,
at least, is punished through Pepa's final dismissal of him and his
relegation to the strident Paulina. But the punishment is apparently a
long time coming, and meanwhile he leaves a trail of unhappy
women in his wake, not only Pepa but Lucía, whom he has driven
mad. His son Carlos appears at first glance more sympathetic,
because of his domineering fiancée and handsome if slightly
dishevelled appearance, plus his collaboration with the women in
their schemes (notably in the distribution of the spiked gazpacho).
But as his mother remarks, he is just like his father in his attentions to
Candela, taking the opportunity to fondle her backside and breast as
he retrieves her after her failed suicide bid; and he continues to grope
her even as Marisa lies unconscious nearby. Another apparently
sympathetic man, the wonderful Mambo taxi driver (Guillermo
Montesinos), who gladly ferries Pepa from place to place as she
attempts to sort out her problems and offers all the services he can (to
the extent of supplying eye drops for her), ultimately shows a superficial
attitude towards women when he says they are easy to handle, and
eventually refuses angrily to help Pepa any further after being shot at
during the chase to the airport (we should note that the fear of being
shot does not deter Pepa from continuing to pursue Lucía).

    When talking about María in *Matador* I used the concept of the
masquerade as a model for perceptions of women; femininity as a
performance and a façade that becomes indistinguishable from the
woman herself but which causes a certain unease. This concept can
also apply to the women of *Mujeres*, as Girelli has remarked (*19*,
p.254: see above). As Evans comments: 'Both Lucía and Pepa take
part in a masquerade of femininity, thus creating an effect of coolness
and detachment, enabling the viewer more easily to note the extent to
which femininity is defined through artifice and imagery' (*18*, p.70).
But we can also think in terms of a male masquerade, in which
masculinity — and in particular in this film, male sexuality — is also

a performance behind which it is hard to detect a real masculine core. Pepa's dream sequence in which Iván walks along muttering compliments to a series of women exemplifies this idea, since the compliments are ultimately meaningless and there is no feeling behind them. His very job as a dubbing actor adds to this implication of masculinity as a performance or act, as he repeats romantic clichés to a woman whose voice and whose thoughts, significantly, we cannot hear. This concept is reinforced further by the concluding bolero in which a woman sings to her lover 'eres puro teatro', again suggesting masculinity as performance and pretence.

Masculinity, then, is not a solid rock of patriarchy against which women will inevitably destroy themselves but is itself a fragile construct that is vulnerable. As Evans observes: 'masculinity is comically represented as also on the verge if not of nervous breakdown then at least of structural fatigue' (*18*, p.40). If women are hysterical, patriarchal rationality is no longer the powerful counterweight it was. As Pepa remarks, it is easier to understand how a motorbike works — a machine, deriving from reason — than a man, implying that men are not susceptible to rational scrutiny (and also that it women who apply such reason). I noted above how hysteria in women traditionally required some form of male control in order that they did not cross moral boundaries. Whether we agree with this need for such control or not, it is clear that men are not up to the task.

The voice and (lack of) communication

The need for women to live independently of men is further underscored by the lack of communication there appears to be between men and women. Almodóvar stresses this early on in the film, as Pepa and Iván dub *Johnny Guitar* but at different times, so that instead of dialogue we have a disjointed conversation that makes no sense. As Smith comments, 'the staggering of the two [dubbing] sequences suggests the lack of reciprocity between the lovers: each addresses only the screen' (*3*, p.95). Similarly, the messages that each leaves to the other on the answering machine emphasise the lack of a dialogue between the two: each addresses only a machine and not the other person directly. Indeed, there is no direct dialogue between Pepa and Iván until the final scene at the airport; and when Iván suggests that they talk Pepa tells him it is too late. But she also tells him that all she wanted to do was talk to him, suggesting communication as her ultimate desire that is never to be fulfilled. By the time she has the chance to talk, she no longer has the desire.

From this it would also seem that men — or Iván, at least — do not have the desire to communicate that women do. This may initially appear ironic, since Iván's charm for women lies above all in his voice, to the extent that it sends Lucía mad again when she hears his voice on television. But his voice, while a device of enchantment, is not one of communication: Iván never communicates with any woman directly (except when he is on the receiving end of Paulina's hectoring, an appropriate comeuppance). Smith argues that Iván, with his microphone, flirting with a line of women (in Pepa's dream), and his disembodied voice on phone messages, has become nothing more than Voice — and even this is finally unpersuasive, since Pepa abandons him (*3*, p.95). Epps echoes this idea, pointing out that although Iván ostensibly speaks to all the women in the dream sequence, he is only talking to himself, into the microphone (*17*, p.118). And, being in love with his own voice, he is not desperate to have the voices of women intrude (it is notable that of the line of women he addresses in the dream, only the final one answers him back, in a move of comedy designed to puncture Iván's pretensions). Thus as Epps observes, Iván desires not communication but an inability to hear: as his message to Pepa on the cover of her favourite song reads, he never want to *hear* her say she is unhappy (*17*, p.118). This is in fact what transpires, as Iván never gets to hear of Pepa's problems. When Iván does his dubbing in *Johnny Guitar* the original actress Joan Crawford 'moves her lips and keeps silent — a woman beautiful, desirable, mute'. And he does not need Pepa with him to do the scene, 'he needs only himself' (*17*, p.119).

But if the fault of a lack of communication seems to spring from Iván, it is nonetheless one that spreads to others. Pepa's absorption in her own problems renders her deaf to Candela's pleas for help, driving the latter to her suicide bid. Lucía refuses to accept

Pepa's statement that Iván has left her. Candela fails to heed Pepa's instructions to dissimulate when the police arrive, thus nearly giving the game away. A notable sequence that highlights the general lack of reciprocity in the film occurs as Iván attempts to ring Pepa from a phone box, while she walks past him with his suitcase. They do not see each other. Nor does Lucía see Iván, cowering in the phone box, as she walks past to reach Pepa's flat. Pepa ironically manages to convey her feelings about Iván's new woman as she throws objects out of her flat, first hitting Paulina on the back of the neck and then the bonnet of her car — but Pepa remains unaware of the effectiveness of what she has done. One of these objects is Pepa's telephone; and telephones function specifically in the film as symbols of the failure to communicate (as well as a personal reference from Almodóvar, who used to work at the Spanish telephone company Telefónica). The phone is a device to facilitate communication, but the phones of *Mujeres* never enable anybody to connect to anyone else. On the only two occasions that the phone *does* work, it brings trouble. Carlos's call concerning the terrorists merely brings the police to Pepa's flat, while Lucía's phone call to Pepa brings the former to the latter's flat at the same time, with the subsequent confrontation of the women over glasses of gazpacho and the frenzied dash to the airport. The most effective function of the telephone, in fact, is to express Pepa's feelings as she throws it about (including when it lands on Paulina's car). If a lack of communication seems endemic to the characters there is, however, a small sign of hope at the end of the film as Pepa overcomes her troubles and faces her future. She may be alone but finally she is able to talk to somebody, as she and Marisa chat to each other at the end of the film in reciprocal dialogue.

Madrid: an artificial environment

As with all his previous films (and subsequent ones until *Todo sobre mi madre*), Almodóvar uses Madrid as his setting. While in *Laberinto* Madrid functioned as a hedonistic playground, here, as Núria Triana-Toribio argues, Madrid acts as an illustration of contemporary, progressive middle-class values, while nonetheless emphasising a certain measure of artificiality, as with the clearly false backdrop of Madrid behind Pepa's flat (and we should also note the model building of the block of flats where the action takes place; see *7*). Madrid appears unnaturally clean and sanitised, to the extent that we even see the dustmen keeping things clean (*7*, p.183). In this perfect environment 'the characters have no external worries and can concentrate on affairs of the heart' (*7*, p.184). This does not take into account the fleeting shot of the rubbish tip over which Candela climbs to hide the evidence of her relationship (suggesting in passing the sordid reality beneath the façade); but Madrid is primarily a glossy and comfortable place. According to Vidal, Almodóvar deliberately stressed the artificiality of Madrid so as to bring into relief the authenticity of Pepa's feelings.[21] It may, however, serve to blunt the edge of the women's suffering. Into this contemporary bourgeois space Pepa has introduced a veritable jungle of plants as well as rabbits and chickens. Against the artificial backdrop these items are redolent of not only the more authentic feelings that Almodóvar suggested, but also that these feelings are both more primitive and more domestic than the bourgeois gloss.

As harsh economic and social realities do not intrude, people are free to indulge their emotions in comfort (*1*, p.51). Suggestive of this problem is Pepa's well-apportioned flat which is, according to Marvin D'Lugo (*4*, p.140) the only place where she can achieve liberation. Triana-Toribio disagrees, saying the flat is an 'oppressive environment against which Pepa will have to react' (*7*, p.184). The space that Pepa once shared with Iván is subsequently taken over by women (Candela, Marisa, Lucía), and also becomes the place in which difficulties and traumas are resolved. But within this space lurks Carlos, who may sympathise with the women but who shows the same tendency to flirt with and cheat on women as his father did. The flat thus functions ambiguously.

What is lost from the Madrid of *Laberinto* is a sense of collage in which people compose their lives out of a jumble of sometimes disparate cultural scraps. It has also lost the recognisable landmarks such as the Segovia bridge of *Matador*. Spanish specificity to this

---

[21] Vidal, p.226.

extent has been lost, the only clear marker of Spain now being the gazpacho (which induces sleep due to the fact that Pepa has spiked it with sleeping pills). This brings us back to the American style of the film noted earlier. There is in a sense a certain amount of irony in the fact that *Mujeres* helped to establish Almodóvar as the quint-essentially Spanish director, since in this film the location could be anywhere.

Style

Girelli comments that: 'construction and artificiality are some of the film's underlying themes; centred as it is upon female characters, it pointedly places them at the heart of a world whose fabrication is constantly made visible under the surface' (*19*, p.254). Pepa reflects the sense of artificiality and façade through her use of clothes. Smith links this use to narcissism, as she frequently changes her clothes (parodied by Lucía's similar attention to dress, though with unintentionally hilarious results: see *3*, pp.96–97). These ideas might suggest once again a lack of sympathy for women: is Almodóvar poking fun at them? This coincides with the fragmentation of women that occurs in the title credits, that also emphasises women's fashions (implying that they are cracking up behind the elegant façade). Yet there is surely a form of sensuous pleasure in the women's clothing and look. Smith argues that we too can take pleasure from this while simultaneously acknowledging the retrograde implications. Thus we experience the pleasure of kitsch with Lucía's dated fashions that nonetheless signify her inability to develop and mature. But the use of fashion contributes to the sense of artificiality and masquerade, as Pepa constructs herself over and over again as a chic, confident woman despite the traumas she suffers. The use of fashion allows Almodóvar the opportunity to display not only his taste for kitsch (particularly with Lucía's clothes, but also in the retro fashions displayed in the opening credits) but for colour, with Pepa's varied reds, while Lucía's final costume of baby pink matched with a childish handbag contrasts with her murderous intent. Colour appears elsewhere, in the blue shade over the telephone booth used by both Iván and Pepa, the reds of Pepa's telephone and the gazpacho, the bright orange of Pepa's note to Iván, the blue and white stripes of Candela's outfit, the yellow hair of the taxi driver. (It is striking that Candela uses a blue telephone that matches her outfit to call Pepa, and Pepa answers using a red telephone that matches *her* outfit.) *Mujeres* is saturated in colour in ways that sometimes border on the ridiculous (such as the overly pink face of the pharmacist trying a facial treatment).

In terms of music, the most striking elements of the soundtrack are the opening song, Lola Beltrán's 'Soy infeliz', and the closing song 'Teatro' by La Lupe, which emphasise melodrama (see 5, p.94). Girelli (*19*, p.254) suggests that the use of Beltrán's 'Soy infeliz' adds meaning to the montage of the opening credits that suggest female fragmentation. The music recurs midway through the film as Pepa discards Iván's suitcase, and coincides with Iván's farewell message: there is an added irony in that Pepa literally dispenses with the first song when she throws the record out of the window, hitting on the head the woman partly responsible for her unhappiness. Having discarded this first song, she is now ready to move on to the sense of the closing song, that men are nothing more than performance. Other soundtrack elements also suggest melodrama and tension, such as the suspense music as Pepa waits outside Lucía's flat or the face-off between Pepa and Lucía over glasses of gazpacho. Occasionally Almodóvar blends melodrama and comedy, as in the use of a dramatic string motif from Rimsky-Korsakov's 'Scheherezade' that mimics the shrill tone of the telephone operator insisting that Pepa return the piece of paper that carries Iván's number, and a haunting violin melody from the same classic piece is used as Pepa broods on her balcony. More music from Rimsky-Korsakov occurs in the combined melodrama and humour of the conflagration Pepa wreaks on her bed. Mambo music is used as a point of comic characterisation for the taxi driver, but also suggests the drama of the chase. The melodramatic mood is enhanced by the use of extreme close-ups, of Pepa's feet and ears, of Iván's mouth and so on, hinting at the overwhelming power of personal emotions. This strength of emotion would continue in Almodóvar's later films while the use of comedy, so prominent here, would prove more intermittent.

5. Carne trémula

By the time of *Carne trémula* (1997), Almodóvar had been making films for well over fifteen years. The heady days of the *movida* were now long past, as the excesses of that time began to catch up with those who participated in it. Almodóvar himself, with box office success and an Oscar nomination, was in danger of becoming an establishment figure, the sole contemporary Spanish director with whom international audiences might be familiar, and thus a symbol worldwide of what Spanish cinema was. Maybe now was the time for the *movida*'s *enfant terrible* to grow up a little: at any rate, by the time of *Carne trémula* there is a discernible shift in Almodóvar's films to a comparatively sober tone. As we shall see in the chapters on *Todo sobre mi madre* and *Hable con ella,* this also on occasion would facilitate a darker tone as well as a more serious one.

This shift did not occur immediately. The films immediately following *Mujeres al borde de un ataque de nervios* demonstrate close links with his preceding work rather than the simple recycling of the more mainstream comedy that made *Mujeres* so successful. *¡Átame!* (1990) was perhaps the most controversial of these, in which

Almodóvar provides an unusually sympathetic depiction of an obsessive man who captures, imprisons and ties up the woman of his obsessions, until eventually she falls in love with him. This is another of the director's portraits of pathological people, but one that caused some controversy precisely because of the potential to read into the film negative attitudes to women, and a more lenient approach as regards crimes committed on women. *Tacones lejanos* (1991) is more reminiscent of *Mujeres*, foregrounding the melodramatic trials of a mother and daughter and the importance of the mother-daughter bond over and above relationships with men. It also reintroduces a nod towards the blurring of gender boundaries with the cross-dressing performer Femme Letal, though as in *Laberinto* this gives way to the possibility of the heterosexual happy ending as Femme Letal is revealed to be the local magistrate who wishes for a relationship with the central female character. *Kika* (1993) chronicles the traumas of a beautician called Kika, who, like Pepa and her female cohort in *Mujeres*, suffers as a result of the sexual selfishness of men. This film, too, proved controversial because of a rape scene played in comic overtones, which drew similar criticism to that of *¡Átame!* The change in Almodóvar's style and pace to a slower, more measured and mature feel dates from the next of his films, *La flor de mi secreto* (1995), the film prior to *Carne trémula*. Here we find none of the frenetic antics of *Mujeres al borde* but instead a focus on the efforts of a writer and middle-aged woman to overcome the loss of love as well as writer's block, to obtain a new and hopeful outlook on life by the end. The orientation towards the fast paced life of young adults changes to the travails and possibilities of middle age. Comedy exists but melodrama is once more to the fore; and the pace of the film is slower.

Further changes also come with *Carne trémula*. The emphasis Almodóvar placed on female characters in so many of his films begins to dissipate somewhat from this point on: while men had been at the centre of *La ley del deseo*, from *Carne trémula* the director puts men centre screen more often, particularly in the later *Hable con ella* and *La mala educación*. *Carne* also introduces an intermittent concern in the films with social themes such as disability and urban deprivation (which we will consider in the course of this chapter). The following film *Todo sobre mi madre* deals with death, motherhood, AIDS, and the downsides of transgressive sexual behaviour, while *Hable con ella* portrays the difficulties of death, loss, and of coping when your loved one is in a coma. While Almodóvar still provides depictions of sexual diversity, sex as a form of pleasure and as a form of violence, and instances of popular and counter cultures, as well as a varied gallery of female characters, the comparative sobriety of theme and style in these later films indicates his development as a director.

  Carne is the only one of Almodóvar's films that is an adaptation, from a novel by British mystery writer Ruth Rendell. It is nonetheless a fairly free adaptation, with a change to a happy ending and a change of setting to Madrid (with landmarks such as the sloping Kio towers in whose shadow the central character Víctor (Liberto Rabal) lives). According to Mark Allinson (*1*, pp.152–53), while Rendell focuses on plot at expense of characters, Almodóvar focuses on characters at expense of plot, which suggests that the mystery element is not the director's primary concern. As Allinson goes on to say, Almodóvar creates more hybrid texts than does Rendell (p.153), which mitigates the sense of a crime thriller. This is not, however, to deny the similarity of the film to a mystery story, in which Almodóvar carefully spaces out the revelation of the crime and its consequences, revealing the guilty party more or less in the middle of the film, then revealing the motive for the crime, and subsequently offering a climactic form of confrontation with guns. We initially think Víctor is guilty of the crime, then we discover Sancho (José Sancho) is guilty, but in turn he commits the crime only because David's (Javier Bardem) betrayal led him to do so. Almodóvar in fact provides us with a clue early on that we should not take the appearance of guilt for granted, by way of the film playing on the television in Elena's (Francesca Neri) flat, Luis Buñuel's *Ensayo de un crimen* (1955). In Buñuel's film the protagonist dreams of committing many crimes in his mind, but never actually commits them in real life, although ironically his selected victims all die by some other means. The young protagonist of *Ensayo* in the clip believes he is responsible for the shooting of his nursemaid, but the shot in fact came from elsewhere. The point is reinforced by the discrepancy of the two women who let David and Sancho into Elena's building: one called the police because she heard shooting, while her companion insists it was only the TV.

History and politics

Carne is also unusual in its reference to history. Previously Almodóvar's work deliberately neglected to explore the traumas of the past beyond the parodic reference to the historically divided Spain in *Matador*. The opening shots of *Carne*, however, occur against the historical background of the political disturbances and the consequent state of emergency of 1970, when the Franco regime was ailing much as the dictator himself was. The film's opening caption presents the decree with which the state of emergency was announced, and the loss of freedom of speech and movement that this would entail. Life was grim and austere, as we can see from the empty streets of Madrid at night: the Christmas lights are up but the curfew means that nobody is around to appreciate them. The later newsreel sequence in which the baby Víctor is presented with his permanent bus pass is a reminder of the Francoist newsreels through which the regime shaped their version of historical and political events and which cinema audiences were forced to watch. The sequence nonetheless includes a touch of Almodovarian humour in the juxtaposition of a prostitute (Víctor's mother, played by Penélope Cruz) with the dignitaries and worthies, and particularly their wives, who come to visit the baby Víctor and celebrate the unusual circumstances of his birth. We move on rapidly from this historical segment to the main body of the film, which takes place in the 1990s, but at the very end Víctor reminds us of that opening sequence when he tells his unborn child that things are different now from the time when he was born. Now people are free to live without fear. And as if to underline the point we have a Christmas backdrop again, but now the streets are bustling, lively, and full of colour. People are free to come and go as they please.

Carne trémula was made in 1997. In 1996 the long rule of the Socialist party (the Partido Socialista Obrero Español or PSOE) had ended, and there had come to power the right-wing government of the Partido Popular, a party originally known in the early days of democracy as the Alianza Popular. The head of the Alianza Popular when it was first formed was the politician Manuel Fraga, who had been a long-standing member of Franco's regime. It is Fraga's voice we hear on the radio at the beginning of the film, announcing the state of emergency. With the ascension to power in 1996 of a party founded by a Francoist the film hints at the possibility of Spain's historical clock turning back and of the ever-present potential of history to regress to a state of dictatorship and repression. And this idea again relates to the parallels at the beginning and the end, which presents a sense of circularity, of the wheel turning full circle. Events and situations can repeat themselves (like the birth of the two babies in public transport at the beginning and end of *Carne*). While Spain has progressed politically since 1970, the motif of circularity (to be found also in the circular route of the bus on which Víctor travels at the beginning, so that he travels round and round in circles), implies that to go in circles is to make no progress. For all the circularity implied by the film, however, things have changed by the end: the Madrid of the final scene is bright, lively and crowded in contrast to the empty greyness of the opening sequence. The upbeat ending may thus serve as a reminder that, even with the right back in power, Spain is no longer afraid and people should continue to act without fear; and it may also serve as a warning not to go back to those miserable days of 1970. Rikki Morgan-Tamosunas stresses the circularity of the film as dominant over any hope of progress, considering Víctor's positive outlook as unreliable and arguing that *Carne* critiques 'a presumed stasis which lurks beneath the surface of the massive changes that have taken place in Spain since the end of the dictatorship. It is a stasis which relates to the inner workings of gender roles and relations […]' (*20*, p.198). But while these possibilities do indeed lurk beneath the surface, the argument for stasis neglects other factors, in particular Víctor's upward mobility which I discuss below.

Men at the centre of the narrative

But what makes *Carne trémula* a more notable step away from
earlier concerns is that this film demonstrates an effort to move away
from the female-centred narratives that made Almodóvar's name
previously, in order to focus on male characters. Although the
subsequent *Todo sobre mi madre* marked a return to female-centred
narratives, the two films that followed that, *Hable con ella* and *La
mala educación*, allowed men to take centre stage once and, more
worryingly, reduced women to often silent bystanders, as I will
discuss in the chapter on *Hable con ella*. In *Carne*, however, we
encounter more complex, nuanced and sympathetic male characters
than in *Mujeres al borde* in which the central male character Iván
serves as little more than a caricatured male villain. *Carne trémula*
provides intricate depictions of the male protagonists Víctor and
David that contrast with the rather flat portrait of the central female
character Elena, a character for whom it is hard to care deeply.
Indeed, we could argue that the interest provided by the main male
characters may distract us from the fact that in the end the woman
they compete for is little more than a cipher rather than the three-
dimensional and quirky female characters of other films. Elena
functions as little more than a prize to be won rather than a person
with her own needs and desires.

Almodóvar's previous work would lead us to expect more
sympathy for those male characters who break from stereotypical
models of masculinity, and to some extent that is what we do find.
But even the character who conforms most closely to the macho
stereotype, Sancho, eventually receives a sympathetic treatment that
coincides once more with Almodóvar's capacity to make us
empathise with pathological characters. Sancho is a wife-beater and
an alcoholic: he assumes his wife Clara's (Ángela Molina)
unfaithfulness (with some justification, although it may be that his
jealousy and violence has driven her to seek comfort in other
relationships — thus his fears are self-fulfilling), and eventually he
shoots her dead before turning the gun on himself. His underlying
motivation is his overly possessive desire for Clara which impels him
to domestic violence. Sancho is also guilty of shooting and crippling

(and thus betraying) his colleague David in the shootout in Elena's flat, though neither David nor the audience realise this for quite a time, as Sancho successfully frames Víctor for the crime. But it is precisely in the middle of the film, as Víctor reveals to David and to us what actually happened, that Almodóvar begins to elicit our sympathy, even as we absorb Sancho's duplicity. We come to realise that the violence stems from Sancho's own vulnerability and his increasing desperation to hang on to his wife, and the fact that David previously betrayed him through an affair with Clara. The scene in Sancho and Clara's flat offers us an unexpected role-reversal, given our knowledge of the character hitherto: Sancho is cooking for Clara in the flat while she sits back on the sofa with a glass of wine. As Sancho talks over his frying pan, we become aware of his powerlessness and the pain of his desire. None of this justifies the violence, but it does complicate a negative reaction. We have here another instance of Almodóvar's appeal for our sympathy towards an otherwise dangerous and threatening character with distorted desires.

Sancho's portrait of the perils of macho masculinity is, however, only a minor note in the film, as the characters of David and Víctor are more to the fore. Both demonstrate the potential that men possess to show traits of care, empathy and gentleness more traditionally associated with the feminine — and yet neither character appears emasculated as a result, even though David, because of his disability after the shooting, is physically impotent. Both Víctor and David are more concerned to give their partners sexual pleasure than simply to ensure their own satisfaction, to the extent that Víctor wishes to take lessons from Clara as to how to give women sexual satisfaction. Víctor's job as a carer for small children is also traditionally feminine employment, but his role at Elena's orphanage seems both effective (his coworkers praise him) and natural (and we should note that he is not the only male worker there).

Unlike Sancho (or Iván in *Mujeres al borde*), both Víctor and David undergo profound changes in their characters, again suggesting that men are not fixed in traditional behaviours but can learn and develop. This is perhaps clearest with Víctor, initially presented (as an adult) as a geeky pizza delivery boy, impossibly

infatuated with Elena after a rather fumbling one-night stand that
merely marks him initially in her mind as sexually inadequate. His
infatuation is underscored by the fact that he does not perceive her
unpleasantness (her irritation and unkindness towards him stem from
her desperation for a drugs fix). The subsequent shooting incident
appears to offer a negative perception of Víctor, as at this point we
do not know of Sancho's duplicity. Once in prison he inspires more
complex reactions. He appears rightly to be paying the penalty for his
crimes, but it is hard not to sympathise as he watches David's
basketball success on the prison TV (a sympathy assisted by the
accompanying song 'Sufre como yo' which expresses all the rage that
Víctor feels). Prison also opens up opportunities to change: he gets a
qualification in education that will allow him to work at Elena's
orphanage, and works out in order to change the shape of his body to
a lither one. Ironically, prison will be the making of Víctor, allowing
him a better future once released and a better chance of sexual
success with women. He is able to overcome his jealousy of David,
and his desire for revenge — he has moved on from the emotions in
which Sancho is imprisoned. And we see him move up, too: the
working-class male can now be upwardly mobile (*1*, pp.53–54).
Víctor initially lives in his squalid flat which is marked for
demolition and which was left to him by his dead mother; but by the
end of the film he has the wealthy Elena for his partner. And by the
end of the film Víctor, once so eager to learn, is now giving
instruction and encouragement as he takes Elena through the correct
breathing exercises for her labour (and even commandeers the help
of the driver taking them to hospital).

　　　David's change and growth as a character is not immediately
apparent in that from the beginning he seems more reasonable and
capable than his partner Sancho, handling the initial standoff with
Víctor with care. His disability might seem an obvious locus of
traumatic change but although David copes with this admirably, there
is no sense of a drastic change in his personality to accompany this.
Like Víctor, his concern during sex is to ensure the satisfaction of his
partner, hence the tender bathroom scene in which an inability to
achieve sexual satisfaction himself does not mean that he will deny it

to his wife. Nonetheless David has changed. The whole chain of events in the film has been set in motion by an event that we do not see, David's affair with Clara which leads Sancho to shoot David and frame Víctor for the crime. David's earlier betrayal of his colleague thus causes the later traumas from which he, Víctor and Elena suffer (though also eventually bringing about Víctor's victory and the prize of Elena). This earlier incident will eventually reveal a more dubious side to David once we find out about it, but we also see his ability to overcome this: while he reacts with anger to the news of Elena's sexual encounter with Víctor, he realises soon enough that he has lost her and, unlike Sancho, is able to let her go and move on with his own life.

The break with older stereotypes of masculine behaviour does not mean that the two men cannot revert to masculine posturing or male bonding, factors which Almodóvar gently parodies in the scene where David goes to confront Víctor in his flat. In the middle of the confrontation (during which David ably asserts masculine power over Víctor by grabbing his crotch) their attention is diverted to the football match playing on Víctor's television, as the frenzied voice of the commentator proclaims a goal. The men immediately drop their posturing in favour of a male bonding moment as they celebrate the goal together. And they then promptly revert to their standoff, Víctor cruelly underlining his physical power by doing a series of rapid pushups while David struggles out of the room in his wheelchair. For an infinitesimal moment, as David attempts to cope with the stairs, we see Víctor's macho mask slip as he wonders whether to go and help his rival, but he reverts to his show of testosterone. This scene, for all its humour, underscores again the notion that even machismo is a more complex phenomenon than the stereotype might lead to suppose, with complex emotions and reactions lurking just beneath the surface.

The male body

While Víctor develops into a caring and sensitive man, his body seems to follow the opposite trajectory. In the early stages of the film we see him first as a new born infant, then as a clumsy, unsophisticated young man with a very ordinary appearance and (according to Elena) no ability whatsoever at sex. But prison makes a harder man of him: he shaves his hair and begins to work out. The editing of the film implies that he starts training in response to seeing David's athletic display at wheelchair basketball: we first see him in prison watching the basketball match on TV, and then we cut to the sequence in which he is training both his mind and his body. Gradually he becomes stronger (as evidenced later by the boxes of fish he carries for his job), and by the end of the film he is good enough at sex to make Elena pregnant, this being the ultimate sign of a potent male body. Much of this honing of the male body arises from the sense of macho competition, although it is also worth remembering that the earlier moment of male bonding with David also occurs in response to a performing male body, the footballer who scored the goal. But Víctor is spurred on to continue in his training beyond prison precisely through the sense of competition with David: one of the first things he sees on his release from prison is a poster of David playing basketball, captioned by the single word 'champion', implying not only David's sporting success but his winning of everything Víctor desires.

Víctor's body is also on display as an object of erotic desire. We literally see more of him than any other character, not only when he is with Clara in his own home, but the full frontal shot where he dashes into a kitchen in flames. Traditionally in cinema it is the female body which is displayed (clothed or otherwise) as the erotic object of desire of the audience's gaze, implicitly male,[22] but here it is the male body thus displayed as an object of desire. Víctor as object of the gaze is stressed still further by the fact that David spies on and photographs him. To have the man as the object of our gaze feminises him and makes him vulnerable. These shots, then,

---

[22] This theory of the audience gaze as inherently male derives from Laura Mulvey, 'Visual Pleasure and Narrative Cinema', *Screen* 16. 3 (1975), 6–18. Her argument that films position us as inherently male and heterosexual (and thus desiring of women as objects) when watching films, regardless of our actual identities, has since been challenged or modified (and Mulvey herself came to revise it).

counteract the idea of the male body as simply a sign of masculine strength. The scene of the kitchen fire, however, may offer us a voyeuristic shot of the nude male body but in fact this shot is on the surface devoid of erotic overtones: there are few occasions that override the erotic potential of the nude body on display but the emergency of a house fire is certainly one of them. Any sexual readings of this scene are inherent in us the audience rather than the scene in itself: thus Almodóvar plays with our perceptions of nudity and the body.

If we consider the film as a contest of male bodies, then we might assume that Víctor will win it not only from his very name but also that he does not have the disadvantage of being confined to a wheelchair. However, David's disability does not mean that he counts himself out of the competition, nor does Víctor neglect him as a threat. His reaction to David's athletic prowess on TV is not one of pity for a disabled man but of jealous rage at a rival, his apparent defeat emphasised further by the 'champion' poster. David's energetic body has implications for the way in which disability is portrayed in the film, which I discuss in more detail below. Almodóvar explicitly draws attention to the disabled body: something that the able-bodied tend to prefer to forget and ignore. Here we may simply note that being disabled does not prevent David from competing for Elena on level ground. But David has his vulnerabilities, too: he becomes jealous of Víctor as Víctor is of him, and spies on Víctor and Clara in a voyeuristic fashion. Voyeurism suggests simultaneously power by spying on someone and acquiring knowledge of them that they do not know you have. But it also implies powerlessness, spying on someone else's affair because you yourself cannot act in the same way. This conceptual impotence mirrors David's real impotence: while both men appear to be able to satisfy Elena, only Víctor can impregnate her. It also hints at the idea posited by Rikki Morgan-Tamosunas (*20*, pp.190–91) of David's body as symbolic of the castrated male that reflects the deeper masculine anxieties and frailties she perceives in the film.

Chris Perriam (*21*, p.105) has argued that Almodóvar twists both plot and title of the Ruth Rendell novel to 'make his film a film

about the body', reinforcing Allinson's comment quoted above the
film concerns character over plot. This applies not only to displaying
Liberto Rabal's body (as Víctor) for pleasure, and questioning our
attitudes to disability, but other aspects such as the physical depiction
of the labour at the beginning of the film. There is also the issue of
damage to the body in the form of domestic violence, with the shot of
Clara's black eye as she looks out of the window of her home. The
jealous reaction of Sancho is likewise written on David's body
through his injury and leads to Víctor's body being caged in prison.
The body in *Carne trémula* becomes not simply a thing to be
admired and enjoyed but a vulnerable entity, always under the threat
of being rendered powerless. Even the lithest body, like Víctor's, can
be undermined by a simple blow to the testicles. The healthy body is
not therefore to be automatically equated with power.

Disability and class

One of the most notable elements of *Carne trémula* is Almodóvar's
look at an aspect of disability: the wheelchair-bound David and his
attempt to overcome his handicap. Although, as we shall see, there
are downsides to this portrayal of disability (notably its intersection
with matters of class and consequent access to resources),
Almodóvar is nonetheless to be lauded for illustrating the capacity to
live a fairly full life with a disability, for promoting the integration of
the disabled into society, and indeed for providing a depiction of
disability at all, since the disabled are on the whole notably absent
from cinema screens. Almodóvar demonstrates further possibilities
for the disabled body in its capacity for ballet (the shots of
synchronised movement as the basketball team practice are like a
dance) and for sex (David can still give sexual satisfaction). As the
poster featuring David proclaims, a disabled person can still be a
champion (and not incidentally can be used in an advertising
campaign even though advertising normally features bodies that are
all too perfect). An additional aspect of the portrayal of disability
comes with the use of Javier Bardem in the role of David. Perriam
(*21*, p.109) reminds us how the character of David maps on to
Bardem's past history playing overly machismo roles that explore the

destructive side of masculinity, as in *Huevos de oro* (José Juan Bigas Luna, 1993); and this might also apply to Bigas's Lunas's preceding film *Jamón jamón* of 1992, with Bardem as a comically thrusting young macho. Bardem's previous roles emphasised masculinity as physicality; so that his performance here not only signals a change of direction for the actor but nuances the perception of the character of David for any audience member with an awareness of Bardem's earlier roles, offering up a suggestion of masculine power behind the apparently disabled body.

One of the difficulties with Almodóvar's portrait of the disabled David is the fact that we do not see him coming to terms with his disability, since an ellipsis in the action means that the film cuts from the moment of the shooting to the imprisoned Víctor jealously watching a triumphant and athletic David winning at wheelchair basketball — and dancing the night away with his wife Elena afterwards. This fairly easy transition has the advantage of suggesting that disability is no barrier to achieving success and the good life — and the girl as well. It does, however, fudge over the traumas associated in learning to live with disability, traumas which may continue throughout the disabled person's life but which must be particularly acute when a formerly able-bodied person becomes incapacitated in adult life. We could say that David adjusts to disability rather too easily. On the other hand, the film is really Víctor's story rather than David's, told primarily if not solely from his point of view. And from Víctor's point of view the disability is refreshingly irrelevant — David is a man to be envied, not pitied. Clearly the disabled body is not a negligible element of male competition.

But when it comes to disability, it helps to be well off. Much of David's ability to adapt to life in a wheelchair has come about because he has become rather wealthy through marriage to Elena (an heiress). As a result, their home has gadgets such as the stairlift which facilitate his movement. As neither he nor his wife have to earn a living, David has plenty of time to devote himself to basketball practice, and there is no suggestion of the struggle that disabled people often encounter in finding work and in adapting themselves to it. He also has an expensive car in which to travel round (while Víctor is still reliant on his bus pass), so that he does not have to tackle public transport; although, as the film shows graphically enough, it is still a struggle to get from the car to the wheelchair. The scene where David attempts this is in fact the start of his move on to Víctor's terrain, and we begin to realise the extent to which wealth might have eased David's path. In the wastelands around Víctor's home, the wheelchair encounters many obstacles in its way such as stones, while the ultimate obstacle of the steps to Víctor's front door reveals that nobody thought of adapting these homes for the disabled and, under the threat of eviction notices, nobody is going to alter this any time soon. In an area where no one is wealthy, the path for the disabled is not smooth going.

Urban deprivation and the difficulties encountered by the less wealthy to participate in a society that values wealth and consumerism form, like the matter of disability, part of an emphasis in Almodóvar's later work on social issues. Madrid is the setting of all Almodóvar's films until *Todo sobre mi madre*, but the city has functioned mostly as a playground for the young, where money is not a problem (as in *Laberinto de pasiones*) or a glossy bourgeois background for emotional trauma (as in *Mujeres al borde*). Only once previously has the director chosen to show the economic trauma of trying to survive in Madrid, in *¿Qué he hecho yo para merecer esto?* In *Carne trémula* we still find bourgeois backdrops such as David and Elena's flat, but we also now see Madrid as also a site of poverty cheek by jowl with the trappings of wealth. Víctor's home lies under the shadow of the slanting Kio towers, now a noted landmark on the Madrid skyline, and built partly out of oil revenues. These ironic phallic symbols merely mock the deprivation and powerlessness of those who live beneath them. Víctor is due to be evicted even from this poor space, in order to make way for a new road named after the Príncipe de Asturias (the title given to the Spanish heir to the throne), implying that the poor must always give way to the rich and the privileged. However, in the Madrid of the democratic era class structures are more fluid, in contrast to Madrid under Franco. Víctor's mother is an uneducated and innumerate prostitute who does not rise any higher in the social scale despite the momentary attention lavished on her in the newsreel stories. Although she bequeaths money to her son, the home she leaves him is dilapidated and unfurnished. Her son, in the democratic era, moves up the social scale despite a spell in prison. Indeed prison has much to do with his rehabilitation, providing him with an education and thus better job prospects than before he went in, when he delivered pizzas (*1*, pp.53–54).

Linked to the question of wealth is the theme of charity work, also highlighted in the film. Elena's involvement in the children's home is her own form of character development from the unpleasant junkie of the shooting scene. Her participation in charity is very much tied to her own wealth: she can do this because she has the money (and other workers at the home see her as a cash cow to be milked for funds). Nonetheless participation is not confined to the rich; and Víctor, too, finds a role there despite his lower class status. Other social issues touched on in the film are domestic violence and overindulgence in alcohol. Alcohol in the film leads not to pleasure but to violence and destruction: Sancho has drunk heavily before the opening incident where he shoots David, while alcohol appears to fuel his violence towards Clara as well as her inability to leave him. Similarly, drug-taking is no longer simply the recreational affair it was in films such as *La ley del deseo*. While David and Elena companionably smoke a joint together, we also have Elena's unpleasant attitude while waiting for her dealer. Her attitude has its humour, particularly in her request for a chocolate bar along with her drugs, but she initially inspires little sympathy (which perhaps prevents us from identifying with her point of view later in the film). And her drug-deprived temper has its own part to play in the escalating violence in her flat.

Style

The newer stress on social concerns has its counterpart in a more muted comic approach. The madcap antics of the early *Laberinto* are not possible when time is taken to address social issues such as the consequences of drug and alcohol consumption. More pointed emphasis on humour would also have detracted from the positive portrayal of disability that Almodóvar is clearly keen to provide. Humour in consequence becomes gentle, such as the male bonding over football. Other light touches of humour include the jumble of things that Víctor learns in prison such as Bulgarian and Bible verses (which Víctor quotes inappropriately at times), which initially serves to disguise the direct value that his prison education will provide — gaining voluntary work and eventually Elena and upward mobility. Other humorous elements serve to point up the theme, such as the incongruous birth of Víctor beneath the Christmas star which nonetheless serves to point to his function as the eventual victor, the chosen one; or the incongruous juxtaposition of his mother with the Francoist worthies that hints at his later upward mobility.

The humour is also more muted because of the running thread of the film's function as a crime film, rather than comedy or melodrama, although crime and melodrama share an impulse towards overly dramatic climaxes, particularly when the crimes of the thriller are crimes of passion. Thriller and melodrama combine in the deaths of Clara and Sancho resulting from the latter's uncontrollable emotions. Almodóvar's intermittent taste for psychopaths means that in the relevant films there is always a mystery to be uncovered, a point that coincides with the fact that this is an adaptation of a mystery novel. But in contrast to the mystery underlying *Matador*, for example, *Carne trémula* offers twists and turns in the plot so that new layers of mystery arise and are resolved. The thriller aspect may underlie the more subdued style of the film in contrast to previous ones, although the link between the two is not inevitable, given that the later *La mala educación* mixes the noir thriller with the flamboyance of drag performance. Many of the stylistic elements mentioned in the discussion of earlier films play little part here: there is not the former emphasis on colour, fashion or alternative lifestyles (although Almodóvar occasionally plays with touches of colour, such as in the scene of Sancho and Clara at home in which Clara wears and is framed by red tones while Sancho has blue, suggesting their ultimate incompatibility). Style as a whole is more restrained, in keeping with the idea that Almodóvar has calmed down for a more mature approach (though in fact some films that come after this one, such as *La mala educación* and *Volver* demonstrate that the director has not simply discarded the more spectacular style elements with the years). *Carne*'s style is stripped to the bare essentials. Almodóvar nonetheless retains one stylistic hallmark in his use of music, although even here he adds new dimensions such as the music of the Afro Celt Sound System to which the disabled basketball team move, thus stressing their agile and almost balletic qualities. But older, more Hispanic song styles are prominent in the use of highly charged flamenco music 'El Rosario de mi madre' as David stalks Víctor in a jealous rage, the lament 'Ay mi perro' as David and Sancho patrol the streets in their car, a song which Sancho specifically relates to his own situation; and more particularly 'Sufre como yo' by Albert Plà which, as Allinson notes (*1*, p.201) expresses to the full Víctor's feelings, no additional information being necessary. The cheesiness of the incidental music that featured in an early film such as *Laberinto* has now given way to a more conventional use of orchestral music that highlights emotions and links scenes in a standard way of mainstream film, such as the music that bridges Sancho and Clara's final quarrel in their flat with that of David and Elena, or the closing exchange of dialogue between Víctor and Sancho as the latter dies. This again indicates how far Almodóvar has moved from the more makeshift and parodic style of his early films.

6. Todo sobre mi madre

Todo sobre mi madre, the film that followed *Carne trémula*, could be regarded as the culmination of all Almodóvar's previous styles and themes to date, with throwbacks to the *movida* and the emphasis on women combined with the newer stress on social problems. It was certainly the height of his domestic and international success: *Todo sobre mi madre* finally earned Almodóvar an Oscar in 2000 for Best Foreign Language Film as well as seven awards in the Spanish equivalent, the Goyas. It also, however, points forward to subsequent work, and particularly *Hable con ella*, in its confrontation of trauma and tragedy. The initial subject matter of *Todo sobre mi madre* — a mother's loss of her son — is so harrowing that it is difficult to believe that Almodóvar can inject any humour, or any of his trademark kitsch and flamboyance, into such material. Nonetheless part of Almodóvar's achievement with the film is precisely the fact that he manages to do just that while never diminishing our sympathy for the pain that the central character Manuela (Cecilia Roth) experiences on the death of her son Esteban (Eloy Azorín).

The film is once more centred on women, in contrast to the male-centred narrative of *Carne trémula*, and very reminiscent of *Mujeres al borde* in which women learn to live without men, as they do here. The character of Agrado (Antonia San Juan) also reminds us of the transsexual Tina of *La ley del deseo*, and her colourful clothing and distinctive, humorous and sympathetic approach to her own transsexuality compare with the kaleidoscope of colour and sexuality of early films. We return to the love of kitsch as for instance in the loud patterned wallpaper in Manuela's Barcelona flat. The concern for social issues that came later with films such as *Carne trémula* has not, however, been dropped (and it continues in films subsequent to *Todo*). In the early films, the cultural effervescence of the *movida* embraced a philosophy of anything goes, of excess as the norm, but here we see that excess has consequences. Nina (Candela Peña), a drug addict, is both unpleasant and unreliable, hurting her lover Huma Rojo (Marisa Paredes) and frequently endangering the running of the production of Tennessee Williams's *A Streetcar Named Desire*. Manuela and Huma also descend into a hell-like scenario in search of Nina, exposing the sordid reality behind the search for a fix. Compare this to the casual and humorous treatment of drugs at the fashion show in *Matador*. Drugs also overlap with AIDS and HIV and the dangers of unsafe sex: Lola (Toni Cantó) dies of AIDS as a direct result of the life he has led, and in addition he infects Rosa (Penélope Cruz) and their son (also Esteban). And the pleasure of sex has been replaced by the rather depressing scene of the prostitutes in Barcelona, with cars circling round them, looking at the merchandise. Sex is now dangerous rather than pleasurable, as the initial assault on Agrado suggests as well as the death of Rosa. Finally, the film looks at not only the trauma of coming to terms with the loss of a loved one, but also the importance of organ donation.

But the film is not only a tragedy but another example of melodrama, full of coincidences and twists, such as Manuela and Rosa sharing the same father of their child, the meeting with Huma, the fact that Manuela begins and ends the story with a son called Esteban, and the play *Streetcar* as a backdrop to key moments in Manuela's life, such as meeting the father of her son, and the son's subsequent death. Like *Carne trémula*, the film possesses a circularity which nonetheless allows people scope to move on and improve their lives. The film also ends happily with baby Esteban's triumph over the AIDS virus. Indeed, it is this miraculous ending that perhaps is most implausible part of the film, as the ends are tied up too neatly and pleasantly to be convincing, most of all in terms of the baby's recovery but also in his grandmother's (Rosa María Sardá) new acceptance of him (a transformation from her earlier hostility that we never see) and the disappearance of Nina, the least pleasant character. Too many people change too rapidly for the ending to avoid a sense of rushing to finish the film and tidy the story away. On the other hand, melodrama can sometimes do just that in an effort to complete everybody's own individual story and leave no loose ends hanging: although much of the film emphasises tragedy rather than melodrama, the latter is the more appropriate term for the film's ending. The baby's conquest of disease may also arguably symbolise the idea that the central characters (or at least those that survive till the end of the film) have themselves exorcised the demons that afflicted them (and which drove the plot) and are now able to move on to new lives and thus new stories beyond this film.

Mothers and families

Todo sobre mi madre functions as a homage to mothers, as the end credit suggests — and in particular to Almodóvar's own mother, who had died before the film was released. (The director's mother appeared in cameo roles in a few of his films, for instance playing the part of the elderly newsreader who announces the story of the Shi'ite terrorists in *Mujeres al borde*.) In particular it celebrates a particular and popular notion of what it is to be a mother, for ever caring and self-sacrificing. Manuela epitomises this notion, taking care of all the lost and damaged characters who cross her path, offering nurture to Agrado and Rosa, taking care of Huma, trying to reconcile Rosa and her mother, and finally looking after baby Esteban and becoming his substitute mother in the process. On one level this is a very positive valorisation that stresses the importance of the mothering role, though there are also negative connotations such as the insistence on the traditional role of motherhood for women that differs from the emphasis on female independence in *Mujeres al borde*. The film thus has scope for a conservative interpretation. This interpretation gains support in turn from the contrast between Manuela and Rosa's mother, who seems harsh and cold towards her daughter (though they do draw closer as Rosa spends her final days in hospital). Rosa instinctively turns to Manuela rather than to her mother for help. The implication is that all good mothers should be like Manuela without probing into the reasons why Rosa's mother is as she is. The need to care for a sick husband and earn money for the family through fraudulent activity — the forging of Chagall paintings — might be enough to turn many a parent sour.

Sentimentality over maternal, nurturing values fits in with Almodóvar's tendency to melodrama, as many melodramas deal with the emotional trials of motherhood, usually emphasising maternal abnegation. The maternal melodrama also stresses motherhood as a form of suffering. Many of the women of *Todo* suffer, and Manuela above all. This risks the suggestion of suffering as an inevitable part of women's lot rather than something to be resisted: it also implies that any suffering is worth it for the sake of the child — the child justifies the suffering. It is interesting, in this light, to think of the character Agrado in relation to the other women. Allinson has highlighted her as the prime focus for comedy in a film with a great deal of trauma in it (*1*, p.135), but there is a link here to the fact that she is a deliberately constructed woman, so that pleasure and a carefree heart are only available to such as her. Agrado herself has certainly suffered; ill-treated by Lola, beaten up by her client, and insensitively exploited by the actor Mario (Carlos Lozano). But it seems that only Agrado gets access to humour: the other women can only aspire to suffering, and can laugh only when Agrado is with them.

Motherhood, then, requires self-abnegation and a disregard for one's own needs in the face of the needs of others. It does not, however, require a traditional nuclear family of husband and one's own children to exercise the mothering function. Stephen Maddison has suggested that motherhood is not biological but a chosen role

(*26*, p.279). And as Vilma Navarro-Daniels suggests, when Manuela loses her first family (her son Esteban) she goes to Barcelona and forms a new family (*28*). This compares to 'constructed' families offered in earlier Almodóvar films such *La ley del deseo* with its family unit of a homosexual man, his transsexual sister, and the child of her lesbian lover. Manuela's new family includes Rosa, Agrado and Huma Rojo. Her mothering embraces the transsexuality of Agrado, the lesbianism of Huma, and the sexual transgression of the nun Rosa that has endangered her life. It accepts AIDS and HIV (as Manuela first cares for HIV-positive Rosa, then in turn her son Esteban). Mother love accepts all. The role of Stella in *A Streetcar Named Desire* furthers suggests surrogate as well as real motherhood: Stella acting as carer for her sister Blanche as well as her newborn child. It is no wonder that Manuela plays the role more convincingly than Nina does, or that she slips back into the role so easily when she has not acted it for years.

Although Manuela functions as the centrepiece of the mothering theme, we can find motifs elsewhere that reinforce it, including the failed mother-daughter relationships of Rosa and her mother, and also to some extent the relationship between Huma and Nina, in which Huma constantly watches over and worries about Nina, and accepts her on any terms. The new production for which Huma begins rehearsals towards the end of the film is a performance deriving from two plays of Federico García Lorca. Lorca's *Yerma* centres on a woman who is so undone by the fact that she cannot have children, that she ends the play killing her husband, while in his *Bodas de sangre* a mother cries out at the death of her sons. Ernesto Acevedo-Muñoz (*22*, p.29) reads the shots of the trains going through the tunnels in terms of childbirth rather than the usual suggestion of penile penetration as used previously in films (a clear example being the train entering the tunnel in Alfred Hitchcock's *North by Northwest*). Even the passing shots of Barcelona's famous cathedral emphasises the point, given its name of the Sagrada Familia or Holy Family.

The roles of the women, and above all that of the mother, ironically leave very little room for men. In contrast to *Carne trémula*, in which the men formed the centre of the action while the main female character acted as little more than a cipher, here it is the men who are little more than vague sketches, ciphers in their turn. The men who figure in the orbit around Manuela are either dead or damaged: her son Esteban dies, Lola is also dying, and Rosa's father suffers from senile dementia. Even the baby is HIV-positive until his miraculous recovery (this may suggest a miracle on another level: men normally do not thrive so well in this environment). Almodóvar has also replaced the bonding scene between David and Víctor in *Carne trémula* with the bonding of four women in Manuela's flat, a more sustained and more nurturing scene in which Manuela ensures that Huma will not be without some form of care while she herself looks after Rosa — at and the same time she ensures Agrado both a job and an opportunity to shine. Allinson comments on the fact that women find their greatest satisfaction in their relationships with each other, and do not look to men for emotional satisfaction (*1*, pp.86–87). Men, in this film, simply have no real function, they are an absence. There is no place for them in this community of nurture. After *Todo* Almodóvar would offer a very different perspective on men and the caring role, as we shall see in the chapter on *Hable con ella*. After the heavy emphasis on women in *Todo*, both *Hable con ella* and *La mala educación* push women to the background: only with the subsequent *Volver* does the director return to the idea of women as a community caring for each other.

Intertextuality

A particularly marked feature of *Todo sobre mi madre* is its intertextuality, wherein the film explicitly refers to other texts, plays and films, in order to enhance its own meaning. Almodóvar used intertextual references previously in *Mujeres al borde* with knowing quotation from Alfred Hitchcock's *Rear Window* and Jean Negulesco's *How to Marry a Millionaire*, the latter underscoring the notion of *Mujeres* as a screwball comedy reminiscent of the American ones of the 1950s; while the *Rear Window* reference may simply be added 'for fun'. More integral to the plot and the themes of *Mujeres* was Almodóvar's use of Nicholas Ray's *Johnny Guitar* both as plot device but also to illuminate the dysfunctional relationship between Pepa and Iván. In subsequent work Almodóvar refers to other more generic texts such as reality TV shows in *Kika*, or uses the occasional quotation from another film such as *Ensayo de un crimen* in *Carne trémula* (itself an adaptation of the Ruth Rendell novel and thus an explicit reference to it). Nonetheless with *Todo sobre mi madre* Almodóvar's intertextuality would reach its zenith, with the incorporation into the film of scenes from *A Streetcar Named Desire*, Lorca's plays, the work of Truman Capote and the film *All About Eve* (Joseph L. Mankiewicz, 1950). Maddison notes that the intertextual references in *Todo* provide links to gay and camp identities as well as to the relation between gay male identities and women, through *Streetcar*, Capote, Bette Davis (a gay icon) and Lorca. He observes more generally a link between camp identities and an appreciation of motherhood (*26*, pp.277–78). *Todo* certainly acts at least as an observation of some of the terms of reference of these identities; and these intertextual allusions undergird the familiar fluidity in Almodóvar's film of sexual and gender roles.

Of all these texts the use of *A Streetcar Named Desire* is the most sustained. Manuela claims that the play has shaped her life, and she knows the script by heart not simply because she has previously acted in it, but because these lines form the start of her own story which she knows so well. The play brought Manuela together with her husband (who subsequently became Lola): as they played the married couple Stella and Stanley in Williams's drama, so they marry each other in real life. And as in the play they are mismatched — Stanley's rejection of Stella's sister Blanche results in Stella's rejection of him — so Manuela and Lola are mismatched. Nonetheless, despite the mismatch, the union of both couples results in a baby. While Manuela abandons Lola, fleeing to Madrid without divulging her secret that she is pregnant, both Lola and the play continue to haunt her. When her son Esteban notes that all the photos of Manuela are torn down one side, as if to indicate that there is another half of her life missing, it suggests that there is another story to be told, and that story starts with *Streetcar*. The attendance of Manuela and Esteban at a performance of the play occurs at the same time as Manuela promises to tell her son about his missing father. *Streetcar* also marks the beginning and end of Esteban's life: if earlier it brought his parents together, his enthusiasm for the play and for the performance of Huma as Blanche, leads directly to his death under the wheels of a car. Manuela's original performance as Stella might also act as a rehearsal for the subsequent and recurring roles of mothering she is called upon to perform. Just as she can slip back into the role of Stella so easily, having been a mother for some years as I observed above, so we can perceive her mothering role as stemming from her performance as Stella, the fact that she plays the part better than Nina again suggesting the role as a clue to Manuela's character. On the other hand, we might remember that subsequent to her own performance as Stella, Nina leaves Huma, gets married and has a child of her own, suggesting an echo of the role's capacity to induce motherhood. *Streetcar* also acts as a script for Huma Rojo: at one point she actually quotes the play, saying to Manuela, when she agrees to help her look for Nina, that she has always depended on the kindness of strangers.

Maddison points to Almodóvar's alteration and reworking of *Streetcar* as implying that women have choices outside the traditional heterosexual relationship dissected by the play. He observes that Almodóvar alters the play to have Stella move on from the heterosexual relationship she shared with Stanley, and that in the same way Manuela moves on from her past life, involved with men, to form alternative bonds with women (though we should also bear in mind that eventually Manuela abandons all the women in order to forge a mothering bond with a male baby) (*26*, p.268). It is interesting to think about the implications of these changes: Manuela was able to substitute for Nina because she had already learnt the part of Stella — but which part? Williams's original conception or Almodóvar's reworking? If she has learnt the original, then she has had to modify the script she learnt for the submissive heterosexual woman, in order to play new versions of the mothering that entail independence of men. We should also think of the implications that Esteban/Lola played Stanley, the macho posturing of the part giving way to sexual indeterminacy. Intertextuality does not, then, automatically entail a reverential preservation of the other text but a reinterpretation of it for new times and circumstances.

The play draws the viewer's attention not only to the film as a form of melodrama (in which emotions and traumas are dramatically heightened and even exaggerated), but indeed as an artificial construction of emotion that can nonetheless spill over into real life. This has its parallel in the role-playing concerning organ donation that Manuela does at the hospital. While she performs her part conscientiously enough in rehearsal, nothing perhaps prepares her for having to perform the same role in reality, and the difference between acting and real life is on one level reinforced. She experiences the horror of what she has been playing at for the first time (and her colleagues responsible for arranging the transplant likewise show more emotion than they have done previously, when we see preparations for an organ donation in the opening sequences). And yet on another level this distinction between acting and reality is blurred, since the same doctors of the role play the same parts, with the same lines, in both the role play and the real conversation with Manuela, while Manuela's lines when she discusses the possibility of donating Esteban's organs have been previously scripted for her. She has rehearsed, as it were, for this moment, acting out a part she knows well (just as with her performance as Stella in *Streetcar*). It is worth observing that with the motif of the organ donation role plays Almodóvar refers to his own work as a form of intertextuality: this incident was prefigured in an early scene of *La flor de mi secreto*.

Another text with relevance to *Todo* is the film *All About Eve*. The title of Almodóvar's film deliberately echoes the film of Mankiewicz, a point that is easier to see from English-language culture. The Spanish version of the title of *All About Eve* is *Eva al desnudo* and, as Esteban and Manuela discuss as they sit down to watch it together, this is not an exact translation, which would be *Todo sobre Eva*. The film prompts Manuela to talk about her past as an actress, and provokes Esteban's curiosity as to her earlier life and in particular his missing father. Manuela resembles the film's central character Eve Harrington, the woman who usurps the star (certainly Nina sees it that way when Manuela substitutes for her). But again

Almodóvar does not quote slavishly but adapts these references to his own purposes. While Eve Harrington is a malign character, Manuela adopts a similar role in order to help others rather than further her own purposes. Another form of intertextuality is the fact that Esteban takes the film's title and adapts it for his own writings, and it then becomes the title of the film we are watching. We could at one level say that *Todo* is in fact the realization of Esteban's writings as he ponders about his mother and father in the cafe: he wants to find out about his mother's earlier life and about his father, and *Todo* supplies the narrative he was looking for. Navarro-Daniels (*28*) argues that Esteban converts his mother into a character in his story, and indeed she goes on to describe how Esteban scripts his mother's movie, though this latter point is debateable. Esteban sets the scene and prepares us for the tale to be told but while he might have laid the basis for certain events, such as the community of women that is a more benign version of that of *All About Eve*, some future events are beyond his control entirely. Patrick Paul Garlinger, on the other hand, proposes a link between Esteban and Almodóvar himself as the author of the narrative *Todo sobre mi madre*, which concludes with a dedication to Almodóvar's own mother (*24*, p.127). But Esteban's own life has in a sense been scripted beforehand, as we see in the references to Truman Capote's *Music for Chameleons*. The book is a gift from Manuela to Esteban on his birthday, and his pleasure at the gift reveals it as something close to his heart, a text of significance to him. Manuela reads the opening lines aloud: 'I started writing when I was eight', and Esteban immediately comments that he therefore is not the only one. He is following Capote's trajectory as a writer.

Transplanting and hospitals

Intertextual references arguably act as a form of transplanting: quotations and motifs from earlier texts give new life to later ones and help them to function. Transplantation nonetheless goes on at a more literal level within *Todo*. The film's opening sequences stress the importance of transplantation as a medical resource but also as a traumatic decision for families, as Manuela acts out the part of a grieving mother and then repeats the performance for real. The motif

forms another part of the stress on social concerns in Almodóvar's
later films and, as has already been mentioned, is also a quotation
from the earlier *La flor de mi secreto*. The scene in *La flor* is only
incidental to the earlier film, but as Ryan Prout has elaborated, these
two scenes share a concern for the body of the nation (*29*). In *La flor*
the mother who must make the decision as to whether to donate her
son's organs expresses a rather racist concern as to who will receive
them: she does not want her son's organs inside immigrants (a
comment that flusters the doctors to whom she is talking, offering a
note of rather macabre comedy). This incident highlights the question
of who belongs to the nation, specifically in terms of the body, with
the mother's fear of giving away body parts to those perceived not to
belong to the nation. But as Acevedo-Muñoz comments, the
transplant process in *Todo* unifies disparate parts of a Spanish nation.
Esteban's heart is flown from Madrid to La Coruña in Galicia in the
north, impelling Manuela to go there in search of her son's heart, and
then to Barcelona in search of his father. Here she meets with
Agrado, from Andalusia or the Canary Islands (there is some
disagreement among critics as to which). Manuela and Lola are
themselves originally from Argentina (as is Cecilia Roth, the actress
who plays Manuela), suggesting that someone has to come in from
outside to bring the country together through her person (see *22*). We
could also argue that the involvement of a Latin American also
reflects the fact that Latin Americans have immigrated to Spain and
form part of its population. If, earlier, the mother of *La flor*
expressed a concern as to who belonged to the Spanish nation, then
Todo responds to this by suggesting immigrants as an essential part
of Spain.

   Transplanting can also be understood in more figurative terms,
as the transfer of roles. While the first Esteban's heart is transplanted,
his quest for the past is also transferred to his mother, who goes in
search of the father he himself was looking for. If, as we saw earlier,
the mothering role is something that can be chosen and adopted, then
so can it be transferred. Rosa transfers the care of her own Esteban to
Manuela (to say nothing of the role of her own mother); Rosa's
mother passes over care of her own child to Manuela as well. The

theatrical role of Stella is also passed from Nina to Manuela. Manuela exchanges one son for another when she goes to see Lola and introduces him to his new son while informing him of the first Esteban: the names of the two sons are also transferable, and come originally from their father. And Manuela connives in her own transplantation when she suggests that Agrado replaces her as Huma's dresser and carer.

With the great capacity for transplantation and transfer that the film reveals, there is a risk of confusion of identity, a lack of awareness of where one person ends and another begins, or what defines somebody as an individual. Manuela demonstrates this confusion when she follows her son's heart to La Coruña: only it is not her son's heart anymore but part of a totally distinct person of whom Manuela knows nothing. On the other hand, the grafting of other parts on to a person's body may contribute to the formation of that person's identity, as Agrado's monologue at the theatre suggests. Agrado takes great pleasure in her 'faked' body, and invites us to share her pleasure with her ability to entertain others with her story of how she came to be faked that way (just as she enjoys wearing a copy of a Chanel suit). Agrado has literally re-constructed herself, but she claims this reconstruction to be the real her. The fake is the reality. Where, then, does authenticity lie? To complicate the matter still further, Lola also has transformed herself through the acquisition of breasts but, as Manuela recounts to Rosa, she stayed with Lola because, as she observes, her husband had not changed all that much despite this major physical transformation (to say nothing of a new name). The essential identity remains unchanged. Falsification can be negative: Rosa's mother's works at painting counterfeit Chagalls (to Rosa's disgust), and her fakes parallel the label that Navarro-Daniels gives her of a faked mother (*28*), as she is not the caring mother that Manuela is. And yet fakery is not necessarily to be seen as simply negative but, as Agrado understands it, a resource that can be utilised to achieve one's authentic personality. As Garlinger puts it: 'As much as Agrado makes fun of herself in an excessive, theatrical manner she is, in the end, profoundly *sincere* [...] her avowal of sentiment about her body is sincere' (*24*, p.123). Authenticity, then, lies in choosing to be true to oneself; and successful transplanting or transfer will only work if the grafting coincides with the person's true nature. That is why Manuela successfully takes on transferred mothering roles, while the belated adoption of a more concerned maternal persona by Rosa's mother, as Rosa lies in hospital, does not 'take' as successfully.

Transplanting may resolve some bodily deficiencies such as the diseased heart of the man in La Coruña who receives Esteban's heart, but other illnesses remain; and *Todo sobre mi madre* is suffused with an ambience of sickness. We have already seen how the men of the film are dead or damaged: we can also say that they are sick, and their sickness comes to affect or even infect the women. Lola is the clearest example of this, infecting both Rosa and their baby; but Rosa's father's illness also comes to infect the whole family, which becomes distorted as a result of the need to care for him. But sickness originates from the women, too, as Rosa's hypertension indicates: it is the combination of her own sick body with pregnancy and HIV infection that kills her. (A flash of Almodóvar's social concern can be perceived here as Manuela lectures Rosa for her irresponsible sexual behaviour and Rosa subsequently requests an AIDS test.) Manuela's mothering role includes care for the sick, not only the major responsibility of looking after Rosa during her pregnancy, and later the nursing of the baby Esteban (to the extent that she actually helps him on his way to a cure), but also patching up a battered Agrado after the latter was attacked by a client during her work as a prostitute. But maternal care is not always sufficient to repair the damaged body. If the body and identity are open to the possibility of transplants and grafts, this also suggests that it is mutable, equally open to the potential for disintegration and decay. The fragility of the body was already implied in *Carne trémula* with David's disabled body: it becomes more pronounced here and in the next film *Hable con ella*, where damage renders the brain inert so that people exist in body but not in mind, their identity thus in jeopardy.

Almodóvar's interest in the sick and damaged body appears linked to a small obsession with hospitals which flashed briefly across *La flor de mi secreto* and is granted more concerted screen coverage in *Todo* and *Hable con ella*. Hospitals stand most obviously for healing, but they are also the place of transplantation, the refashioning of the body, the renewal of life, but also the home of the sick. They are the place where sickness and health meet. Almodóvar posits this from the outset with the opening credit sequence in which we watch hospital machinery trace out the information of life and death across the screen. Like Huma's theatre, the hospitals we see in Madrid and Barcelona offer stages in which death is rehearsed: Manuela's imitations of a bereaved parent are not only dry-runs for her real performance after her son's death, but also demonstrate how life and death issues are replayed over and over again within the hospital. Heart to heart talks are also facilitated by the hospital: it is here that we finally discover the history behind Esteban's birth and Manuela's flight to Madrid, as she recounts it to Rosa.

Style

Despite the grim subject matter of the film, it is not devoid of the humour and quirkiness that by now have become a familiar part of Almodóvar's oeuvre, which work to lighten an atmosphere which might otherwise become unbearably tragic and hard to watch. Much of this humour revolves around the delightful eccentricities of Agrado, most obviously her comic monologue which tells us of how she came to be the way she is. But the director offers other light touches of humour in the dialogues between Manuela and Rosa: when Rosa presumes that the change in Manuela's husband is simply a loss of love, Manuela's beautifully understated reply, 'el cambio era más bien físico' is a subtly humorous prelude to the information about Lola's breast implants that follows. Almodóvar also undercuts the seriousness of Rosa's confession of pregnancy by Lola by the fact that Manuela, who hears the confession, is eating biscuits at the time, and expresses her anger at Rosa through a mouthful of biscuit crumbs; and he also undermines Agrado's exaggerated desire to please by the cold response of a man who delivers flowers to her.

In terms of the film's look, we have already noted a return to Almodóvar's delight in kitsch and vibrant reds after the comparatively sober look of *Carne trémula*. Most striking is the crazy retro wallpaper of Manuela's flat in Barcelona. We have to remember that this is not her choice: her flat in Madrid looks very different (though its warm red and orange tones reflect its owner's personality); but the change in décor may imply the revolution that Manuela's life has undergone. Instead of the neat and orderly Madrid world in which she held control, and the contained private life with her son, now her Barcelona flat forms the stage on which a variety of zany characters cross her life. The flat functions in a manner reminiscent of *Mujeres al borde*, in which women come together to share and solve their problems, but now the décor is at odds with the seriousness of the problems to be solved this time, as opposed to the problems of the bourgeois at play, in clean middle-class surroundings, that we saw in the earlier film. Good taste now suggests coldness, as in the décor of Rosa's middle-class home with her chilly mother at its centre (and also its falseness, given that it is full of fake pictures). Another example of the significance of décor is Agrado's flat, a mixture of things that suggests her own body, made up of different implants. It also mixes colours and styles, suggesting the sympathy between Agrado and Manuela through their parallel décor as well as the vibrancy of both women. Almodóvar's trademark red is again to the fore, from Manuela's raincoat to Huma's hair (and her name) and Agrado's Chanel suit. Allinson also notes the use of blue, particularly in relation to the play (*1*, p.184), though when Manuela substitutes for Nina Almodóvar emphasises red rather than Nina's blue. Thus the move to more serious themes does not preclude the continuation of the colourful style of the early films. It is tempting to connect the return to more vivid colours with a return to female-centred narratives within the film after the male-driven story of *Carne trémula*; and certainly when we turn to Almodóvar's next film *Hable con ella* the use of vibrant colour will have diminished with a return to a male-dominated narrative.

A specific feature of the film is the use of mirrors in the theatre, reinforcing the theme of performance (particularly adopting and perfecting roles). But it is also used, as Allinson notes, as a device for the characters to communicate with themselves, and discover some sort of truth about themselves: though as he also observes, Mario looks at it just to check he looks attractive, in contrast to the women's self-analysis and search for truth (*1*, p.191). It could in fact be argued that Mario does in fact affirm, if he does not actively discover, this truth about himself, confirming his vanity. After all these actions also communicate to us the audience. When the women stand by mirrors, however, their reflection is often repeated, suggesting their greater complexity than that of a character such as Mario. They are also seen in mirrors together, suggesting complicity, shared interests and the potential exchange of roles. Thus in one scene Huma turns from the mirror to Manuela to pass over the maternal role of care for Nina.

One stylistic element that is much diminished this time round is the music, which consists primarily of the musical score of Alberto Iglesias. The use of Hispanic song to express emotion in a melodramatic fashion is perhaps less appropriate here as we have moved to a large extent beyond melodrama to tragedy. There is no longer the need to use music to express emotion, as happened with the songs of *Carne trémula*, as emotion is now too self-evident to require it: music, melodrama and tragedy only come together as Manuela finally confesses to Lola the truth about their son. Although, as we saw earlier, Almodóvar takes us on a tour of Spain, its musical heart has been removed from this film much as Esteban's has. Cultural markers in *Todo* now are visual rather than aural. The attenuation of the music might be ascribable to the female-dominated narrative as the predominance of vivid colour is. As we shall see in the discussion of *Hable con ella*, music returns to the fore as part of an emphasis on performance that is bound up with a masculine difficulty in expressing emotion that consequently relies on women to perform emotion on behalf of men. The female characters of *Todo* have far less difficulty in telling each other, and the audience, how they feel, and do not need the assistance of music.

7. Hable con ella

After the overwhelming success of the female-centred narrative of *Todo sobre mi madre*, Almodóvar reverted back to the focus on men, seen earlier in *Carne trémula*, to produce a film with two strong male roles in *Hable con ella*. *Hable*, along with the film that followed after, *La mala educación*, bring men centre screen and focus on some of the dilemmas that men must solve. While *La mala educación* deals with homosexual desire, *Hable* deals with homosociality. Homosociality is concerned with close male bonds that do not automatically entail a homosexual element (although such an element might be latent within a homosocial situation). As we shall see in due course, homosociality carries with it the implication of the exclusion of women, so that Almodóvar presents the opposite scenario to that of *Todo sobre mi madre* in which women formed their own community of mutual support in which men had no place.

With both *Hable* and *La mala educación* Almodóvar also moved away for a brief period from his familiar stable of actors to use new faces. Such a move is not perhaps surprising: since most of the director's films used dominant female characters, the switch to male protagonists inevitably required different actors. Likewise, the inertness for much of the film of the central women indicates a move away from familiar Almodóvar actresses who had previously played stronger and more active women. With both *Todo* and *Hable*, however, Almodóvar draws on an Argentinian actor (Cecilia Roth in the case of *Todo* and Darío Grandinetti for *Hable*) and fits the character the actor plays to the country. In both films reference is made to the character's nationality. Thus we have a link between the two films in that somebody comes in from outside and immerses him or herself in solving the problems of others, and in the course of doing so resolves his or her own difficulties.

Sympathy for the devil: Benigno as psychopath

Hable con ella provoked a certain amount of controversy once more for the depiction of rape and violence against women. The earlier rape scenes of *Matador* and *Kika*, with their touches of black comedy, made and still make some viewers more than a little uncomfortable; while the growing affection between abductor and victim in *¡Átame!* caused a furore against this sympathetic portrait of an obsessive stalker. *Hable* also includes the rape of the comatose Alicia (Leonor Watling) by her nurse Benigno (Javier Cámara): it is rape since Alicia is in no position to give consent, and it is also an abuse of Benigno's role as carer. The incident is, however, offered to us in an apparently sympathetic light, helped by the fact that for once we do not see the rape take place. It occurs offscreen, covered over by the interpolated silent film; and only with Alicia's subsequent pregnancy does the rape come to light. But it is also the culmination of Benigno's obsessive love for Alicia which has induced him to take on the job of her nurse in the first place; and his obsession, perceived through the friendly eyes of Marco (Darío Grandinetti), the film's other central character, comes across to us in turn as romantic. His name, too, suggests he is a positive character, and not a psychopath. When, on discovery of Alicia's pregnancy, Benigno is accused of being subnormal, we recoil at the brutality of this cruel description even if we ourselves have previously wondered about the nature of Benigno's obsession. Benigno has a further ally in his colleague Rosa

(Mariola Fuentes), who shows friendliness towards him in contrast to the jokes made at his expense by other nurses, and who helps Marco to track down Benigno after the latter's imprisonment.

As noted in the discussions of *Matador* and *Carne trémula*, Almodóvar has demonstrated an intermittent taste for pathological characters who are presented to us with a certain degree of sympathy: María and Diego in *Matador*, Sancho in *Carne*, the murderous lover Antonio in *La ley del deseo* and the abductor Ricky of *¡Átame!* *Carne trémula*, as observed earlier, marked a move towards more male-centred narratives. As a part of this move, the male psychopath moves centre stage as a character we are encouraged to view positively — with problematic and complex results. Benigno in *Hable con ella* is the most complex and perhaps the most troublesome example of this — precisely because he is such an engaging character. The phenomenon reappears in Almodóvar's next film *La mala educación*, in which the abusive ex-priest Berenguer, responsible for the sexual molestation of Ignacio as a child and the expulsion of Enrique from school, also rather surprisingly draws our sympathy. As he is ruthlessly cast aside by Ignacio's brother Juan it is hard not to feel sorry for him as he weeps in the rain — while the victim of the abuse turns out to be an exceedingly unpleasant and selfish character.

Benigno's story, when reduced to brute facts, can easily be perceived as highly negative. He becomes obsessed with Alicia to the extent of spying on and stalking her: he then takes advantage of her comatose state to rape and impregnate her. An explanation for such psychopathic behaviour is readily to hand in Benigno's relationship with his mother, a close, caring relationship that all too easily gives rise to the idea of a dominating mother and consequent homo-sexuality. This is the explanation that Alicia's psychiatrist father falls for when Benigno arranges to consult him (simply as an excuse to get inside Alicia's home and explore): this motif reminds us of Almodóvar's dismissal of psychoanalysis in *Laberinto de pasiones*. It may also be an explanation that we and Marco accept initially when we are introduced to Benigno, who occupies a stereotypically female profession (nursing) and who demonstrates excellent grooming skills.

Almodóvar teaches us the danger of resorting to clichés about sexual orientation when assessing people; for in fact other dangers such as Benigno's sexual obsession may thus go unnoticed. And yet, once we realise where Benigno's interests really lie, our possible identification with him and his story might make us relieved that Alicia's father settles for the explanation of homosexuality, his suspicions having been momentarily roused by the sight of the devotion with which Benigno massages Alicia's thighs.

From the beginning of the film, in fact, Almodóvar problematises easy assumptions about sexual orientation with the very first shots of Marco and Benigno, together in the same frame, as they watch the ballet of the opening sequence. It is Marco (whose heterosexuality is swiftly proved soon afterwards with his rapid involvement with Lydia) who has tears streaming down his face, showing emotion typified as traditionally feminine, while Benigno notices Marco's reaction but does not react the same way himself. Benigno is indeed sufficiently struck by the unusual sight of a man crying at a ballet performance to recognise Marco when he turns up at the hospital. On the other hand, the carer with apparent markers of homosexuality turns out to be the rapist, the aggressor against women. At an early stage, then, Almodóvar demonstrates to us that the clichéd markers of sexual identity cannot act as an adequate guide for us in this film at least.

Almodóvar complicates our capacity to distance ourselves from characters who perform actions we find abhorrent. Although we become aware at a comparatively early stage that Benigno is a little too obsessed with Alicia, the news of the rape and pregnancy come as a shock, because by then we have already been encouraged to share with Marco in the growing friendship between the two men. It becomes hard for us to revise our views of the cuddly and sensitive Benigno, and Almodóvar pushes us instead towards sympathising with the psychopath, making him seem warm and human. An awkward twist in considering Benigno's rape is its potential contribution to Alicia recovering consciousness. When the rape is discovered and reported, and Benigno imprisoned, Alicia disappears from our view, and we do not know what has happened to her until

Marco, having taken up residence in Benigno's flat (and spying very much in the manner of Benigno) discovers that Alicia has recovered consciousness and is sitting in Katerina's (Geraldine Chaplin) dance studio. If the rape and the pregnancy triggered Alicia's recovery, how are we to evaluate events? Benigno has helped to heal her, a fundamental part of his role as a nurse; and while his rape of her is a violent assault on her being, it also re-establishes that very being as viable rather than simply reduced to a vegetative state.

Another point in Benigno's favour has been remarked upon by John Gibbs, who observes that Benigno endows Alicia with individuality even while she is comatose, rather than treating her as simply an inert body. This mitigates against a view of Benigno as simply a psychopath (*31*, pp.61–62). Thus he talks to her; and although his conversations appear no more than monologues, he himself assumes a certain amount of reciprocity, as when he comments to Katerina that Alicia finds interesting a description of a dance. And while his dedication to her favourite pursuits, dance and silent film, might be thought merely to reflect his all-absorbing obsession, he is keen to share his experiences with her as if she possessed sufficient awareness to appreciate the vicarious feelings he offers her. On another level we can also say that Benigno maintains her interests, the interests that give some insight into her personality, when Alicia herself cannot do so. As Gibbs also notes, Benigno's treatment of Alicia as a subject, an active person in her own right, contrasts to Marco's initially treating her as an object when he comes in and stares as her naked breasts while she lies comatose (*31*, p.63–64).

The most overwhelming element of acceptance of Benigno and his deeds comes with Marco's friendship. I go on to discuss the meaning of this friendship, key to the entire film, below. At this point in the argument, however, it is vital to reaffirm how crucial Marco is for any sympathy we ourselves feel towards Benigno. Although Marco earlier tried to reason Benigno out of his obsession and subsequently is duly horrified by what his friend has done, he immediately decides to help him. From the moment they meet each other again in Segovia prison, Marco shows no further condemnation and supports Benigno in any way he can. Two elements from this point on go further to encourage us to see Benigno in a sympathetic light. Firstly, the misguided judgement Marco shows in deceiving Benigno about the fate of Alicia (allowing him to believe that she remains in a coma) leads directly to Benigno's suicide. It is hard not to wish subsequently, along with Marco, that he had told the truth so that Benigno would have lived; and our potential sorrow at this tragic mistake may lead us to view Benigno with compassion. The second element consists of Marco's substitution for Benigno in the pursuit of Alicia. Marco moves into his friend's flat and by an extraordinary coincidence looks out of the flat window to see Alicia returned to full consciousness, sitting in the dance studio. He watches Alicia in the same way that Benigno did in his turn. When he finally meets Alicia, he does so in the theatre, watching a dance performance that again moves him to tears: we have come full circle from the beginning, when Benigno first saw Marco crying at another dance recital. What brings Marco and Alicia together in the end is their link to Benigno, and this link ensures the presumed happy ending as a new chapter opens in the lives of the two survivors, explicitly proclaimed in the final caption 'Marco y Alicia'. Marco affirms Benigno's love for Alicia by taking over his role as watcher and eventually, we must suppose, as lover. The actions of Benigno have brought the two together in belated happiness, which again gives those actions a more sympathetic gloss. The force of the happy ending does not necessarily reflect on Benigno with total credit, since we could also say that only now, with him out of the way, can Marco find happiness. Alicia herself only comes 'alive' once Benigno has died, thus suggesting the possibility of his malign force over her life.

Whatever our own attitude to Benigno, then, it should be apparent that Almodóvar encourages a great measure of compassion towards Benigno, revealing his personality to be more complex than a simple condemnation would imply. Even if, in the end, we cannot go along with the director in his stance towards his character we should acknowledge that he challenges us to look more closely at a pathological side of life rather than simply dismissing it. The danger may be that he might charm us too much with his sympathetic psychopaths. This is always a possibility when slanting a film from the psychopath's viewpoint: we are faced with the choice of not understanding him or her at all or of understanding all too well. Nonetheless Almodóvar's insistence on complicating our understanding of pathological characters makes it difficult for us to resort to an overly simplistic condemnation.

Male friendship

Hable con ella is divided into chapters ostensibly concerning the relationships of the central male characters with women: Marco and Lydia (Rosario Flores), Benigno and Alicia, Marco and Alicia. The central relationship of the film, that of Benigno and Marco, remains unlabelled in this way, yet the film is primarily about this relationship rather than the others. The friendship between the two men comes about as a result of their men sharing a common situation, watching over and caring for a loved woman. Thus the women bring them together and are the ostensible reason for the friendship, but the women themselves are really absent, present in body but not in consciousness. This scenario to some extent resembles the concept of mimetic triangles posited by René Girard in his work *Deceit, Desire and the Novel*.[23] In Girard's mimetic triangle, two men desire the same woman and become rivals, but their rivalry eventually comes to form a homosocial bond that excludes the woman, as she become merely the excuse for that bond. While Marco and Benigno are not rivals for the same woman (even though Marco eventually desires the woman that Benigno does, this is only after the latter's death), they form a bond because of their desire for a woman that eventually become more important, and indeed more real, than the relationship with these women.

The title of the film is *Hable con ella* but in fact Almodóvar offers us men talking to each other and not to women; men communicating amongst themselves. Perhaps the title can be taken

---

[23] René Girard, *Deceit, Desire and the Novel: Self And Other in Literary Structure*, trans. by Y. Frecerro (Baltimore: Johns Hopkins University Press, 1972).

all too literally to mean 'Talk — with her (present at the time of the conversation, but hardly participating)'. Gibbs notes parallels between Benigno and Marco (*31*, pp.62–63): performing a service for their comatose women, admiring them from afar, a deluded belief that the comatose woman loves them (until Marco, at least, learns different). The two characters also parallel each other in their need for the woman to be silent so that they themselves can talk. The stories that lie behind the two relationships suggest that the relationships cannot work in part because the two men are so busy projecting their own desires on to Lydia and Alicia that they have no time to ponder what the women themselves might say. Thus in the car journey to the bullfight that Marco takes with Lydia, Marco talks so much that he does not give Lydia a chance to say what is really on her mind (the fact that she wants to end the relationship and go back to her former lover). Her subsequent injury in the bullring and her coma mean that she will never be able to say these words for herself; and Marco only learns the truth because the former lover tells her so: again, another man speaks on Lydia's behalf. Benigno, on the other hand, can conduct his one-sided relationship with Alicia precisely because she is not conscious and cannot speak for herself. We observed earlier that Benigno can be perceived in sympathetic terms because he treats her as if she were a conscious being with agency to act, but this does not prevent him from speaking on her behalf to Katerina. Her silence is precisely what gives him licence to speak; he would not really want her to get her voice back. This element of Benigno's character is less sympathetic. The film therefore emphasises much more the question of male bonding and homosociality than men communicating to women. Both Marco and Benigno demonstrate the importance of caring but ironically neither Alicia nor Lydia is in a position to appreciate the men's effort to nurture and express their feelings. The men are, rather, demonstrating to *each other* rather than to the women their capacity to take on the traditionally feminine roles of nursing, care and expressing tenderness. They want dialogue with each other and not with the women.

It thus becomes rather worrying that it is another man to whom Benigno finally appeals for understanding for the rape of Alicia; and the element of care that the men demonstrated towards the women becomes instead a form of nurturing towards each other, inward rather than outward looking. Marco allows Benigno to travel vicariously through his guidebooks (communicating to him through his writing: as far as we know Benigno is the only character who reads Marco's work), while Benigno gives Marco a place to live. More particularly, Marco is the only person who supports Benigno once he is in prison: the only other character from whom Benigno receives any sympathy is Rosa, and her own sympathy remains clandestine and tentative (she does, after all, need to keep her job at the hospital). Marco responds to Benigno's appeal for sympathy and understanding, and in doing so he, a man, countenances the rape of a woman by another man; a more sinister side of male bonding. Almodóvar makes this endorsement palatable precisely because this male/male relationship is the central one of the film so that we get caught up in its development and are thus more inclined to sympathise with Benigno and Marco's points of view. Yet women are again the victim of this male friendship.

If this seems a very negative reading of a friendship that demands our sympathy and dominates the screen, we must also bear in mind that Almodóvar provides both a complex and a warm depiction of heterosexual male friendship that moves the portrayal of men beyond the old stereotypes, and contributes to the director's habit of undercutting of the equation between masculinity and machismo. Unlike *Mujeres al borde*, he does not do this at the expense of the male characters, revealing them to be the root cause of the problems endured by women. Rather, Almodóvar demonstrates the benefits to men of doing without macho behaviour in order to adopt an attitude based on feeling and care, attributes traditionally assigned to women. Marco's frequent tears in response to strong emotions indicate his sensitivity, and he is receptive to Benigno's advice as to how to care for Lydia. In return, he will come to care for and look after Benigno. If, in the end, Marco and Benigno come to care for and look after each other, in this respect they resemble the community of mutual support among women that we found in *Todo sobre mi madre*. In each case, too, the mutual support derives primarily from the inability of the opposite sex to give them such support: if the men of *Todo* cannot return the love of the women because of death or incapacitation such as mental illness, then the women of *Hable* equally cannot return the love of the men because of their comatose state. In each film, then, central characters must turn to members of their own sex in order to find love and affection reciprocated. *Hable con ella* in this regard thus functions as a companion piece to *Todo*, suggesting that men as well as women can engage in mutual help and support.

The silent film

As we have seen, much of the difficulty concerning *Hable* centres on the rape of Alicia. But we never see this pivotal event. Almodóvar hides the rape behind the screen of the silent film *Amante menguante* that Benigno describes to the comatose Alicia: instead of simply hearing Benigno's account of the film we cut to the film itself, which thus becomes a film within a film. The film proves to be a diversion in more ways than one: we become caught up in this new tale, while the main story of the film appears to halt for the digression of the love story of Amparo (Paz Vega) and Alfredo (Fele Martínez). In fact we discover that offscreen the rape has occurred: we cut back to the main story with the discovery of Alicia's pregnancy and the revelation that Benigno is the culprit, a fact which takes us by surprise despite his obsession with her. The sympathy for Benigno that Almodóvar attempts to induce is such that this act is wholly unexpected, as we have already seen; but the romantic nature of the silent film, which Benigno describes almost as an offering of love to Alicia, also disguises the brutality of the act it fronts, thus furthering the sense of shock when we realise the truth.

On the other hand, the silent film does in a sense give us some clue as to what is going on offscreen, since it tells us of the sexual encounter of a couple who appear to be in an impossible relationship (given that Alfredo has shrunk to miniscule size as the result of a science experiment), a situation that parallels the quasi-relationship

of Benigno and Alicia and the sexual encounter that takes place
within this. It is paralleled still further by the fact that the woman
appears to be unconscious. The overwhelming size of Amparo
compared to Alfredo also reflects in a literal fashion the enormous
significance Alicia has for Benigno: she looms overly large in his life
to the extent that, just as Alfredo is willingly absorbed into Amparo's
vagina, Benigno himself is swallowed up by this impossible
relationship (when he thinks he will never see Alicia again he kills
himself, as he can see no further purpose in life).

The giant size of Amparo in comparison to Alfredo provides a
further dimension to the film's consideration of relationships between
men and women, and again this dimension is not totally benign.
Alfredo slips his whole body willingly inside Amparo, as the
culmination of a passionate relationship: and Benigno, as the person
who is reality conveying this story to Alicia and to us, perceives this
act as both right and happy (which is how he perceives his own
sexual encounter). We must not forget that Benigno mediates this
story, so that we have no information about the story beyond what he
tells. But, just as we might not totally share his conviction of the
rightness of his love for Alicia, so we do not need automatically to
perceive the story of Amparo and Alfredo in quite the light that
Benigno does. The contrast in size between Amparo and Alfredo not
only offers an element of comedy (especially when we see them
initially in bed together) but also suggests women as an
overpowering and threatening menace that might crush men: as the
two of them lie side by side, the question arises as to whether
Amparo might roll over and flatten Alfredo. We can in addition also
perceive the danger of women absorbing men, swallowing them, until
the male identity cannot be perceived as separate from the woman's.
The film alludes to the notion of the vagina as potentially castrating,
an idea only emphasised by the close-up of the vagina as Alfredo
enters into it (an effect further underscored when magnified by the
size of the cinema screen). It also acts a reminder of the closing scene
of Luis Buñuel's *El* (1953), as the sexually obsessed protagonist
Francisco, unable to cope with marriage and sexuality, retreats into
madness and into a monastery, where he is last seen as he walks

towards a vagina-like tunnel which is surrounded by foliage reminiscent of pubic hair. Similarly, the shots of Alfredo as he climbs over the lunar landscape of Amparo's body also imply that men are rendered powerless by the strangeness and vastness of this landscape with its mountainous breasts. Both Benigno and Alfredo gladly accept the dominance of the woman, but the ideas expressed here have deep roots in older and negative ideas about women as dangerous to men, devouring and castrating. If this is the case, then Benigno and his alter ego Alfredo reveal their desire as masochistic: they actively desire not so much the woman as to be absorbed by the woman.

Performance

Hable con ella incorporates questions of performance into the film, not only the interpolated story of Amparo and Alfredo, but also dance and the bullfight. The film begins and ends with a dance performance, though the tone of each dance is very different. The opening dance features dancers deliberately hurting themselves, throwing themselves against walls and chairs, offering a sense of masochistic pain. There is, however, a man rushing to remove obstacles from the women's path. This opening dance, from Pina Bausch's Café Müller, prefigures some of the motifs of the film as a whole: the wordless suffering of Lydia and Alicia, the concern of Marco and Benigno to help their women in any way they can. From the very start, then, Almodóvar suggests the motif of men as carers. This scenario moves Marco very much: our first sight of him is as he cries while watching the dance. We will discover later that the dance triggers memories of how he was unable to help his previous lover, an impotence that will be repeated in his relationship with Lydia once she is in a coma. His tears at the dance also indicate his need for performance: his tears appear only in the midst of a performance. Marco, then, experiences the emotions of a love that is powerless to alleviate the suffering of a loved one, but he cannot express it himself. He can only respond when the suffering and care is performed, acted out, by others. The closing dance of the film — once again a dance from Pina Bausch, her *Masurca Fogo* — is of couples dancing in pairs, a sedate but upbeat background to Marco and Alicia finally coming together, a suggestion of pairing off and of ordered, synchronised happiness. Once again, then, the dance acts out the underlying emotions of Marco.

If performance is linked to the expression of emotion it is significant that the central female characters both perform, while the central male characters carry out roles as observers: Benigno as nurse watching over his charge, and Marco as writer looking at the customs of the countries through which he travels. The comas of the women force the men finally to express their own emotions directly. Both Alicia and Lydia are involved in some form of performance, though their activities are very different. Lydia's performance as bullfighter encroaches on traditionally masculine domains, and costs her her life after she is gored in the bullring, sending her into a coma from which she never regains consciousness. It might be argued that this repeats the usual punishment for women who dare to be like men and who must thus be put back in their place: we can compare this with Diego of *Matador*, who survives his goring and develops a teaching career. In addition Alicia, in the apparently gentler (though still strenuous) and more traditionally feminine occupation as a dancer, survives her coma (and perhaps also because she undergoes the female experience of pregnancy). However, we can also view Lydia's participation in the bullfight as another element of Almodóvar as a progressive director, portraying women moving into areas of work and life they had not been allowed to penetrate before. Women have, in fact, now moved into the career of bullfighting in Spain. The director does nonetheless undercut this to some extent by Lydia's reaction to the snake she discovers in her room: the woman who stands firm before the bull cowers at the thought of a reptile. This incident primarily functions to offer a point of comedy as well as to bring Lydia and Marco together. It also serves to suggest Lydia's bullfighting as performance, an act adopted for the occasion. The idea of acting suggests carrying something out, but it can also suggest falsity, a pretence assumed as the need arises. If women act out the emotions, then these performances might be acts in this double sense. On the other hand, the notion of women as performers suggests woman as more active as opposed to the men as passive watchers. The women are rendered inactive only through their comas. This counterbalances the more negative connotation of woman as actors in the sense of falsification.

Alicia also performs, as a dancer, although we never see her performance: at most she is glimpsed in the rehearsal room preparing for a performance. It is worth remembering that it is the sight of Alicia performing that first draws Benigno's attention to her. Indeed, his flat functions on one level as his own private theatre box from which he can watch her performances; and this is a box that Marco will take over and from which he will watch in his turn. It is also significant that Marco and our awareness of her return to consciousness is in Katerina's dance studio as she watches the other dancers wistfully. Her return to her waking life is marked in terms of her desire to participate once more in performance; and the subsequent exercises she undergoes with Katerina similarly prepare her for both life and dance once again.

Julián Daniel Gutiérrez Albilla (*32*, pp.51–53) discusses dance within the film as a way of describing what would otherwise be indescribable, not only in terms of Marco's emotions that he cannot express, but also Benigno's relationship with Alicia (he attends the first Bausch performance as a form of bonding with her), including the unfilmable act of his rape. Gutiérrez Albilla also comments on a dance we never see performed but which Katerina describes, in which female spirits emerge from the body of dead soldiers; he suggests that the choreography 'evokes the blurring of subject and object, self and other, and mortality and immortality' (*32*, p.53). On the other hand, we could also argue from this example that the female dancers will then perform the lives of the dead men, suggesting once more the displacement of male emotion on to others who must perforce perform the emotions on their behalf. This, ironically, implies a reversion to an old stereotype of men as incapable of expressing emotion, something that comes more easily to women, to whom responsibility for emotional expression is delegated.

A different form of performance comes in the middle of the film with the song 'Cucurrucucu Paloma' by Caetano Veloso. The haunting song moves Marco to tears once more. The setting for this performance appears to be a luxurious resort or country club, and the select audience include, for those of us familiar with Almodóvar's work, some of the actors from previous films: the camera picks out Cecilia Roth and Marisa Paredes, fresh from their success in the previous film *Todo sobre mi madre*. This must be an audience of well-to-do people and celebrities, including Lydia. It is significant that Lydia and Marco are not next to each other as they both listen to the song: Lydia sits surrounded by people, looking a little uncomfortable, while Marco stands on the edge of the crowd, until he moves away to hide his tears. The song itself tells of dying from mortal passion and lamentation for a lost love. Veloso's song thus performs the increasing rift that is growing between Lydia and Marco. Previous Almodóvar films have incorporated live music performance as an integral part of the action. The concert in *Laberinto de pasiones* provides the opportunity for Riza to discover his wilder side and for Sexi and Riza to meet. The drag songs of Femme Letal in *Tacones lejanos* also offer the chance for the central characters to meet each other. Here, however, the song is a pointer to a couple drifting apart. Elsewhere, as we have seen previously, songs on the soundtrack also function to express the feelings of the characters: the final passion of the lovers in *Matador*, the jealousy and rage of Víctor in *Carne trémula* or men as nothing but an empty shell in the concluding song of *Mujeres al borde*. For the most part the earlier song acted as a form of emotional discovery, either on the part of the characters or of us, or both. This time, however, there is no discovery except that of Lydia who learns of Marco's inability to help his former lover as she sank into drug addiction, underscoring his later inability to talk to or help Lydia, first in her emotional turmoil and then as she lies in a coma.

Style

Compared with earlier films, *Hable con ella* provides less of the quirky humour and eccentricity which had by now become part of Almodóvar's trademark style. Even *Todo sobre mi madre* lightened the film's generally sombre subject matter with the comic oddities of

Agrado. Here, however, the few overtly humorous episodes, such as Lydia's TV interview or when Marco rescues Lydia from the snake in her house, sit oddly with the film's generally quieter tone. The male bonding that occurs here is of a greater intensity that does not allow for, say, the humour of the bonding moment over a football match between Víctor and David in *Carne trémula*. Even the inter-polated silent film, which starts out with comedy, turns towards drama as Alfredo starts to explore Amparo's body in wonderment. In a similar way the setting offers none of the strong colours that mark the previous films, except perhaps for the pale blue tones of Benigno's hospital uniform; nor do we find anything like the eccentric décor of Manuela's flat in *Todo* or the enjoyment of kitsch as in the early films. Indeed, the black and white of the silent film bleaches *Hable* of colour altogether. The flamboyance (but not the humour) will return in Almodóvar's following film *La mala educación*.

For once, too, Almodóvar does not insist on a specific city (Madrid or Barcelona) as his setting. Although Benigno's flat and the dance studio are clearly in a fairly large city (the red stripe on the taxis in the film would suggest it as Madrid) it remains without identifying landmarks. Similarly, the hospital appears divorced from a large conurbation, and its name, 'del Bosque', evokes a pastoral setting reinforced by glimpses of the countryside that afford a backdrop to the four central characters as they take the sun at the hospital. The only landmark that is clearly identified in the film is Segovia prison where Benigno is eventually incarcerated. Thus, while in *Todo sobre mi madre* Hispanic cultural expression emphasised place and the visual (shots of Barcelona) at the expense of the aural (the generic soundtrack), now the position is different. Place is emptied of specificity while music returns to take up roles that emphasise cultural expression; but now culture is not confined to the Hispanic and hints at other locations (England and Brazil). *Hable* offers us a surprising illusion of travel, therefore, ironic in that we are confined for much of the time in hospital rooms. If the only identifiable place in the film is a prison, a place that functions precisely to deprive people of freedom of movement, then the lack of specificity elsewhere suggests freedom. This underlying sense does much to alleviate the potential for claustrophobia in *Hable*, thus making it more comfortable for us to watch.

Music in *Hable* is associated primarily with performance: we begin with the music of Purcell and conclude with a slow love ballad in English and upbeat Latin guitar music, by way of the Brazilian singer Caetano Veloso halfway through. Almodóvar also provides a Brazilian love song as Lydia fights a bull and Marco watches, implying that at this moment he is falling in love with her. A string soundtrack accompanies the emotional high points of the film (with an added electronic pulse in the scene of Lydia's accident), and provides a sense of urgency as Marco rushes to the prison in an attempt to save Benigno's life. The use of the two different types of music — song as part of performance and incidental orchestral music — is quite distinct, pointing to the former precisely as a form of performance rather than simply a different musical style. The two different forms of music do, however, come together in the string accompaniment to *Amante menguante*, which is also in itself a performance (as a part of a film watched by Benigno), additionally a performance of Benigno's feelings for Alicia *and* incidental music for a film. Such a use of music suggests once again that Almodóvar has developed a good deal in his cinematic approach; but we also may detect a sense of circularity as he returns to the emphasis on music as performance, which also occurred in *Laberinto de pasiones*. Talk of progression, then, should not neglect the continuity of both theme and style that occurs in Almodóvar's work. The style of *Hable* is more restrained than the zany *Laberinto*, but both reveal emotional expression as not simply a matter of personal character but inevitably linked to the culture that surrounds the person.

8. Conclusion

As this book was being written, the nominations for the 2007 Oscars were announced. On its original release in the spring of 2006 Almodóvar's *Volver* was widely tipped to be nominated in the category of Best Film in a Foreign Language. Almost a year later, however, *Volver* was eclipsed at the announcement of the Oscar nominations by a more recent Spanish-language film, Mexican Guillermo del Toro's *El laberinto del fauno*, a fantasy story set against the background of Spain in the aftermath of the Spanish Civil War. While *El laberinto* gained several nominations, *Volver* only received recognition through a nomination for Penélope Cruz for Best Actress.

Almodóvar's marginalisation by del Toro and the recent challenge of the Mexican film industry to the best of cinema made in the Spanish language, as implied by the Oscar nominations, may be more apparent than real. The Almodóvar brothers participated in the production of del Toro's previous film *El espinazo del diablo* (2001), a contribution the latter has gratefully acknowledged: the brothers' production company El Deseo has proved a powerhouse in Spanish-language cinema, which in turn indicates that Pedro's presence is both pervasive and nurturing of the cinema of which he has been in the vanguard. Nonetheless, the Spanish cinema scene has undergone a certain amount of change since Almodóvar first burst on to it, not least an upsurge of new films and directors in the mid 90s in Spain (paralleled a little later in Latin America), and a preference on the part of some of these new directors to make films more aligned with mainstream Hollywood cinema than that of Spain. Del Toro's work may now appear fresher (even though he has been making films for the past fifteen years) than Almodóvar's films. After two and a half decades of directing, Almodóvar's work may be all too familiar, with the consequent danger of taking him for granted.

The possible consequences of Almodóvar's cinematic longevity are suggested in a controversy that arose over *Volver* within British film critique. Peter Matthews's review of *Volver* in the leading British film magazine *Sight and Sound* claimed that Almodóvar was simply recycling his themes and style in a lazy fashion. It contradicted the label of Almodóvar as a women's director, arguing that his films merely flatter women while proving more incisive when dealing with men. Matthews suggested that:

> One can't escape the impression that this adept in effer-
> vescent postmodern whimsy is coasting on the goodwill
> he's built with viewers over 20 years and hoping they
> won't notice how some of the bubbles have gone flat.[24]

A flurry of letters in subsequent issues of *Sight and Sound* defended the director from Matthews's charges, arguing that an auteur such as Almodóvar would inevitably draw on themes and motifs from previous films now and then. The controversy does, however, raise the question: once you have seen one Almodóvar film, have you in effect seen them all?

Those who have worked their way through this guide will foresee that my answer to this latter question must be no. One of the

---

[24] Peter Matthews, 'Lost in La Mancha', *Sight and Sound*, September 1996, 42-43 (p.42).

premises of this book was that Almodóvar's oeuvre has developed and matured over the years: the sobriety of *Hable con ella* is very different from the frenetic pace of *Laberinto de pasiones*. Each film, both those mentioned here and others not covered, repay careful study as something distinct is to be derived from every individual film. On the other hand, the *Sight and Sound* controversy as well as the Oscar nominations suggest that we cannot simply take for granted Almodóvar's status as the greatest and best of Spanish cinema in the democratic era: it needs to be critically rethought as the industrial and cultural contexts change — and as academic thought changes too. However, the very fact that we might be surprised by Almodóvar's comparative neglect at the Oscars, that a film critic is tempted to take pot shots at a director who appears so firmly enthroned on a pedestal, that it is vital to periodically reassess Almodóvar's legacy — all this suggests how crucial that legacy has become to contemporary Spanish cinema. Studying Almodóvar, then, grants us insight into a body of work that has proved to be an essential reference point for Spanish film. But it offers us more than that. Almodóvar helps us tap into the ways in which Spanish culture changed after the transition to democracy. Although his films do not tell the whole story of that transition, or function as documentary evidence of it, they stand as a landmark of Spanish cinema that distinguishes the cinema made in a democratic era from that of the dictatorship, showing filmmakers and cinemagoers that new possibilities had opened up. Spanish cinema and culture has benefited enormously from the director's demonstration of what could be done under democracy.

Beyond the confines of this book, then, the debate about Almodóvar's films may change in unforeseen ways. But Almodóvar will always prove worthy of study. This book is a starting point whereby students can enter into the Almodovarian debate: it is of course by no means the last word on Almodóvar, but neither are the current controversies nor the conferences and copious scholarship that continue to revolve around the director. For the last word on Almodóvar can never be said.

Bibliography

The material written on Almodóvar is becoming ever more copious. The following bibliography is only a selection, emphasizing those books and essays that are likely to be of most help to students.

General

1. Mark Allinson, *A Spanish Labyrinth: The Films of Pedro Almodóvar* (London: I.B. Tauris, 2001). One of the classic texts of Almodóvar criticism. Considers in detail every film as far as *Todo sobre mi madre* (a later Spanish edition of the book also covers *Hable con ella*). The book is laid out in terms of theme and style rather than chronologically.
2. Marvin D'Lugo, *Pedro Almodóvar* (Urbana: University of Illinois Press, 2006). An introductory guide aimed at students, this book is thin on discussion of the early films, but offers more extensive critique of the later films, particularly those that are comparatively neglected such as *La flor de mi secreto*.
3. Paul Julian Smith, *Desire Unlimited: The Cinema of Pedro Almodóvar*, 2nd ed. (London: Verso, 2000). The other classic of Almodóvar criticism, offering an indepth, film-by-film analysis. The first edition covers all the films as far as *Tacones lejanos*, the second also includes review material of the films as far as *Todo sobre mi madre*.
4. Marvin D'Lugo, 'Almodóvar's City of Desire', in *Post-Franco, Postmodern: The Films of Pedro Almodóvar*, eds Barbara Morris and Kathleen Vernon (Westport: Greenwood Press, 1995), pp. 125–44. Discusses the use of setting in Almodóvar's films as far as *Mujeres al borde de un ataque de nervios*, and how Madrid in these films comes to symbolise a break with traditional and Francoist cultures, which distrusted and denigrated the city.
5. Vanessa Knights, 'Queer Pleasures: the Bolero, Camp, and Almodóvar', in *Changing Tunes: The Use of Pre-Existing Music in Film*, eds Phil Powrie and Robynn Stilwell (Aldershot: Ashgate, 2006), pp.91–104. Useful essay that discusses the use of music and song in various Almodóvar films.
6. Ewa Mazierska and Laura Rascaroli, *From Moscow to Madrid: Postmodern Cities, European Cinema* (London: I. B. Tauris, 2005).

Chapter 2 covers Almodóvar's Madrid, with detailed discussion of
Kika and *La flor de mi secreto*.

7. Núria Triana-Toribio, 'Almodóvar's Melodramatic *Mise-en-scène*:
Madrid as Setting for Melodrama', *Bulletin of Hispanic Studies*, 73.2
(1996), 179–89. Discusses the use of Madrid as setting for
Almodóvar's work as far as *Tacones lejanos*, and the function of the
city as the expression of emotional excess.

Laberinto de pasiones

8. James Mandrell, 'Sense and Sensibility, or Latent Heterosexuality and
Labyrinth of Passions', in *Post-Franco, Postmodern: The Films of
Pedro Almodóvar*, eds Barbara Morris and Kathleen Vernon (Westport:
Greenwood Press, 1995), pp.41–57. Begins by considering the
reputation of Almodóvar as a gay director before turning to the
psychoanalytic theme, the exploration of Riza and Sexi's past, and
Riza's flight from homosexuality. Concludes by interpreting the film as
an allegory of the trajectory of Almodóvar's career.

9. Núria Triana-Toribio, 'A Punk Called Pedro: *la movida* in the Films of
Pedro Almodóvar', in *Contemporary Spanish Cultural Studies*, eds
Barry Jordan and Rikki Morgan-Tamosunas, (London: Arnold, 2000),
pp.274–82. Includes a brief but useful discussion of elements of
Laberinto as illustrative of the *movida* more generally.
See also *17*.

Matador

10. Ann Davies, 'The Spanish *Femme Fatale* and the Cinematic
Negotiation of Spanishness', *Studies in Hispanic Cinemas*, 1.1 (2004),
5–16. Includes a discussion of *Matador* in terms of gender and
masquerade as part of a wider study of the *femme fatale* in Spanish
cinema.

11. Peter Evans, 'Almodóvar's *Matador*: Genre, Subjectivity and Desire',
Bulletin of Hispanic Studies, 70.3 (1993), 325–35. Considers *Matador*
in terms of melodrama and the family, before focusing on the
implications of genre on gender, with comparison to *Duel in the Sun*.

12. Dominic Keown, 'Ethics and Aesthetics in Almodóvar's *Matador*', in
Hispanic Studies in Honour of Geoffrey Ribbans, eds Ann L.
Mackenzie and Dorothy Severin (Liverpool: Liverpool University
Press, 1992), pp.345–53. As ethics and aesthetics are mostly implicit in
Keown's article, its title does not give much of a clue as to its valuable
content. Keown perceives the film, and particularly its bullfighting
motif, in terms of myth and religious ritual, and argues for both Eva

and, more surprisingly, María, as less than contemporary independent women. He concludes by suggesting *Matador* as addressing questions of individual freedom even within postmodern irony and self-referentiality (the ethics and aesthetics of the title).

13. Leora Lev, 'Tauromachy as a Spectacle of Gender Revision in *Matador*', in *Post-Franco, Postmodern: The Films of Pedro Almodóvar*, eds Barbara Morris and Kathleen Vernon (Westport: Greenwood Press, 1995), pp. 73–86. After outlining the positioning of gender within the bullfight and its surrounding culture, this article goes on to consider gender indeterminacy and the eventual erasure of feminine difference in the film.

14. Paul Julian Smith, 'Pornography, Masculinity, Homosexuality: Almodóvar's *Matador* and *La ley del deseo*', in *Refiguring Spain: Cinema/Media/Representation*, ed. Marsha Kinder (Durham NC: Duke University Press, 1997), pp.178–95. Uses a comparison of *Matador* and *La ley del deseo* in order to address the question of what it is acceptable to show on screen. The sections on *Matador* emphasise gender and sexual difference.

Mujeres al borde de un ataque de nervios

15. Isolina Ballesteros, *Cine (ins)urgente: textos fílmicos y contextos culturales de la España postfranquista* (Madrid: Fundamentos, 2001). Offers a consideration of accusations of misogyny in *Mujeres* at pp.73–86 and provides a defence against such negative critique, arguing that the film redefines rather than denigrates feminism.

16. Celestino Deleyto, 'Postmodernism and Parody in Pedro Almodóvar's *Mujeres al borde de un ataque de nervios* (1988)', *Forum for Modern Language Studies*, 31.1 (1998), 49–63. Starts by defining the director's films in terms of postmodernism and by presenting parody as a quintessential postmodern art form. Then the article relates *Mujeres* to its American references, and to the theme of dubbing and the voice, with a detailed analysis of the phone-box sequence to illustrate the latter.

17. Brad Epps, 'Figuring Hysteria: Disorder and Desire in Three Films of Pedro Almodóvar', in *Post-Franco, Postmodern: The Films of Pedro Almodóvar*, eds Barbara Morris and Kathleen Vernon (Westport: Greenwood Press, 1995), pp.99–124. Uses a detailed analysis of *Laberinto de pasiones, ¿Que he hecho yo para merecer esto?* and *Mujeres al borde de un ataque de nervios* in order to elaborate the role of hysteria and psychoanalysis in Almodóvar's work. The analysis of *Laberinto* focuses on the character of Fabio and on the occlusion of female and homosexual desire in favour of sex as a violent act. That of

Mujeres stresses the hysteric as a woman in search of a man, and the hysterical consequences of the failure to communicate.

18. Peter Evans, *Women on the Verge of a Nervous Breakdown* (London: British Film Institute, 1996). The most detailed and indispensable account of the film, and its standard reference.

19. Elisabetta Girelli, 'The Power of the Masquerade: *Mujeres al borde de un ataque de nervios* and the Construction of Femininity', *Hispanic Research Journal*, 7.3 (2006), 251–58. Useful critique of the film in terms of the female characters, their use of fashion as a form of masquerade and their attempt to appropriate the male gaze: also touches on aspects of the failure to communicate.

Carne trémula

20. Rikki Morgan-Tamosunas, 'Narrative, Desire and Critical Discourse in Pedro Almodóvar's *Carne trémula* (1997)', *Journal of Iberian and Latin American Studies*, 8.2 (2002), 185–99. Argues that *Carne trémula* suggests circularity and stasis rather than a sense of historical progress. It also discusses the fragility of notions of masculinity within the film.

21. Chris Perriam, *Stars and Masculinities in Spanish Cinema: From Banderas to Bardem* (Oxford: Oxford University Press, 2003). Valuable discussions on the performances of Javier Bardem and Liberto Rabal in *Carne trémula* can be found on pp.104–10 and 185–88.

Todo sobre mi madre

22. Ernesto R. Acevedo-Muñoz, 'The Body and Spain: Pedro Almodóvar's *All About My Mother*', *Quarterly Review of Film and Video*, 21.1 (2004), 25–38. Emphasises the film's theme of nationality, including a reconciliation of all parts of Spain, and also studies theatricality and authenticity.

23. Silvia Colmenero Salgado, *Pedro Almodóvar: Todo sobre mi made* (Barcelona: Paidós, 2001). The most detailed study of *Todo* to date, siting it within the context of Almodóvar's work more generally before embarking on a painstaking analysis of the film.

24. Patrick Paul Garlinger, 'All About Agrado, or the Sincerity of Camp in Almodóvar's *Todo sobre mi madre*', *Journal of Spanish Cultural Studies*, 5.1 (2004), 117–34. Starts by discussing some of the intertextual reference in the film (*All About Eve* and *A Streetcar Named Desire*), then goes on to discuss Agrado in terms of camp, arguing that

her artificiality and theatricality function as a sign of her authenticity. The essay also discusses Esteban in terms of gayness.

25. Marsha Kinder, 'Reinventing the Motherland: Almodóvar's Brain-Dead Trilogy', *Film Quarterly*, 58.2 (2004–5), 9–25. The trilogy concerned are *La flor de mi secreto, Todo sobre mi madre* and *Hable con ella*. Kinder traces the development of the brain-dead motif through the three films chronologically, perceiving it as suggestive of transsubjectivity, a process whereby desiring subjects come to identify with the object of their desire. Kinder also links the idea to contemporary Spanish political history.

26. Stephen Maddison, 'All About Women: Pedro Almodóvar and the Heterosocial Dynamic', *Textal Practice*, 14.2 (2000), 265–84. Considers how *Todo sobre mi madre* structures female identification through the use of *A Streetcar Named Desire* and how female identification in turns functions as a form of gay expression.

27. Susan Martín-Márquez, 'Pedro Almodóvar's Transplants: from *Matador* to *All About My Mother*', *Bulletin of Hispanic Studies*, 81.4 (2004), 497–509. Links feminine identity to maternity in Almodóvar's works, seeing *Todo* as the culmination of this process, with a detailed analysis of the mothering function in this film. Although this process over the course of the director's career is not made clear, the discussion of *Todo* is valuable.

28. Vilma Navarro-Daniels, 'Tejiendo nuevas identidades: la red metaficcional e intertextual en *Todo sobre mi madre* de Pedro Almodóvar', *Ciberletras*, 7 (2002), www.lehman.cuny.edu/faculty/guinazu/ciberletras/v07/navarrodaniels. html (accessed 22 September 2004). Discusses the use of other texts in the film, including links to the architecture of Gaudí and the paintings of Chagall as well as Lorca, *Streetcar* and *All About Eve*.

29. Ryan Prout, 'All About Spain: Transplant and Identity in *La flor de mi secreto* and *Todo sobre mi madre*', *Studies in Hispanic Cinemas*, 1.1 (2004), 43–62. Reviews *La flor* and *Todo* in the context of Spain's transplant system, and relates this to questions of national identity.

Hable con ella

30. Debra Faszer-McMahon, 'Poetry and Postmodernism in Almodóvar's *Hable con ella*', *Anales de la Literatura Española Contemporánea*, 31.1 (2006), 47–70. Analyses the sequences of the dances, the song and the silent film as examples of the poetic that nonetheless blur the boundaries between poetry and narrative. Concludes by positing that communication and language, central elements of the film, inevitably fail to connect people.

31. John Gibbs, 'Filmmakers' Choices', in *Close-Up*, Vol. 1, eds John Gibbs and Douglas Pye (London: Wallflower Press 2006), pp.3–87. Section 4, pp.54–68, deals with *Hable*, offering a detailed close analysis that stresses Benigno as sympathetic.

32. Julián Daniel Gutiérrez Albilla, 'Body, Silence and Movement: Pina Bausch's *Café Müller* in Almodóvar's *Hable con ella*', *Studies in Hispanic Cinemas*, 2.1 (2005), 47–58. Addresses the question of performance, dance and the body in the film.

33. Paul Julian Smith, 'The Emotional Imperative: Almodóvar's *Hable con ella* and Televisión Española's *Cuéntame cómo pasó*', *MLN*, 119.2 (2004), 363–75. The section on *Hable* focuses on emotion and ethics. See also *25*.